CONCEALMENTS & CAPRICHOS

Jerome Rothenberg

SELECTED WORKS BY JEROME ROTHENBERG

POETRY

White Sun Black Sun
The Seven Hells of the Jigoku Zoshi
Sightings I–IX
The Gorky Poems
Between: Poems 1960–1963
Conversations
Sightings & Red Easy a Color
Poems 1964–1967
A Book of Testimony
Poems for the Game of Silence
Poems for the Society of the Mystic Animals
Esther K. Comes to America
Seneca Journal 1: A Poem of Beavers
Poland/1931
The Pirke & the Pearl
The Notebooks
A Seneca Journal
Narratives & Realtheater Pieces
Abulafia's Circles
Vienna Blood
That Dada Strain
New Selected Poems 1970–1985
Khurbn & Other Poems
The Lorca Variations
Gematria
An Oracle for Delfi
Seedings & Other Poems
A Paradise of Poets
A Book of Witness: Spells & Gris-Gris
China Notes
A Book of Concealments
25 Caprichos, After Goya
Gematria Complete

ANTHOLOGIES

Technicians of the Sacred
Shaking the Pumpkin
America a Prophecy
Revolution of the Word
A Big Jewish Book, a.k.a. Exiled in the Word
Symposium of the Whole
A Book of the Book
Poems for the Millennium, volumes 1-3
Shaking the Pumpkin

TRANSLATIONS

New Young German Poets
Hochhuth's The Deputy
Gomringer's Book of Hours & Constellaitons
The 17 Horse Songs of Frank Mitchell
  X–XIII
15 Flower World Variations
Schwitters' Poems Performance Pieces Proses
  Plays Poetics
Lorca's Suites
Nezval's Antilyrik & Other Poems
Picasso's Burial of the Count of Orgaz &
  Other Poems
Writing Through: Translations & Variations

PROSE

Pre-Faces & Other Writings
The Riverside Interview
Poetics & Polemics

For a more complete list, please visit
Jerome Rothenberg's website at:
epc.buffalo.edu/authors/rothenberg

CONCEALMENTS
& CAPRICHOS

Jerome Rothenberg

BLACK WIDOW PRESS
BOSTON, MA

Black Widow Press is an imprint of Commonwealth Books, Inc.,
Boston, MA. Distributed to the trade by NBN (National Book
Network) throughout North America, Canada, and the U.K. All
Black Widow Press books are printed on acid-free paper. Black
Widow Press and its logo are registered trademarks of Common-
wealth Books, Inc.

Joseph S. Phillips and Susan J. Wood, PhD., Publishers
www.blackwidowpress.com

Text and Cover Design: Kerrie Kemperman
Cover Art: *Waiting for Seurat* by Nancy Tobin

ISBN-13: 978-09842640-0-1
ISBN-10: 0-9842640-0-0

Library of Congress Cataloging-in-Publication Data on file

10 9 8 7 6 5 4 3 2 1

Printed in the U.S.A.

ACKNOWLEDGEMENTS

Four of the poems in "A Book of Concealments" originally appeared in *4 poèmes d'un livre des recels,* translated into French by Yves di Manno, Cahiers de la Seine, Paris, 2003. "The Times Are Never Right" was published as a broadside by Brighton Press, San Diego, with art by Ian Tyson, and "A Deep Romantic Chasm" was published as a broadside by Brighton Press in 2007, with art by Bill Kelly. *Concealments* 1 to 25 were published as *A Book of Concealments* by Chax Press in 2004, and *Concealments* 26 to 50 were published as *A Second Book of Concealments* by Veer Books (London) in 2007. A selection of poems was also published as an artist's book, *Romantic Dadas,* by Collectif Génération (Paris) in 2009, and the Postscript to *A Book of Concealments* appeared in a limited sculptural edition from Ian Tyson's ed.it in France. Previous publications in magazines, e-zines, and anthologies include those in *5trope, Barzakh, Big Bridge, Black Renaissance Noire, Bombay Gin, damn the caesars, A Gathering of the Tribes, Golden Handcuffs Review, Helicon* (Israel), *Hunger, Kiosk, Margie Review, Milk, Odradek, PIP (Project for Innovative Poetry), Poem in Your Pocket, Poetry Salzburg Review, Poet's Corner, Skanky Possum, Tin Lustre Mobile, Veer Off, War and Peace Project* (ed. Leslie Scalapino), and *YAWP.*

Earlier versions of segments from the *50 Caprichos* include *25 Caprichos, After Goya* (2004), published by Kadle Books in Spain, with translations into Spanish by Heriberto Yépez, and *Homage to Goya,* with design and images by Ian Tyson, published by Brighton Press, San Diego, in 2008. Publications in magazines and e-zines include *26, Call: A Review, Exquisite Corpse, Fascicle, Festschrift for Clayton Eshleman, FO A RM, The Gertrude Stein Awards for Innovative American Poetry, Golden Handcuffs Review, Lit, Matter, MilPoesias, Octopus, Process,* and *YAWP.*

...for those who went before

WHERE NO FRIEND SURVIVES

From friend to friend
the voice comes,
& the answer
that a stranger overhears
robs him of speech.
The guest is half
oracular.
Nowhere he turns
or runs, caught
in a web
or caught between
two open doors,
is right for him.
The way out west
leads back to Asia,
Asia leads him
into wilderness,
a bitter landscape
where no friend
survives,
no gaze or touch
so tender.
Those who fight
for love,
once living,
know it as a taste,
sweet in the mouth
though distant.
At length, at last,
the friend is double
in your sight,
but turns from you.
The time to come
draws nigh.
And does the poem exist
when there is no one there
to hear it?

20.ii.10

CONTENTS

A BOOK OF CONCEALMENTS

A PRE-FACE

A Book of Concealments and *50 Caprichos, After Goya* are a two-pronged follow-up to an earlier hundred-poem work, *A Book of Witness,* with some notable changes in strategy & composition. In *A Book of Witness,* I was concentrating on the rescue of the first-person voice as our principal instrument of witness—not only the personal "I" but the possibilities of a real if sometimes fictive "I" across a range of experiences, my own & at choice moments those of other, mostly recent poets from whom short & often cryptic phrases were appropriated & put in play. By contrast the poems in *A Book of Concealments* suppress or conceal the witnessing "I" but draw from more distant "romantic" predecessors & from my own accumulated works by collaging as italicized inserts small fragments of poems already written & published, while *50 Caprichos,* written simultaneously, compensates for the largely missing "I" by allowing a give-&-take responsive to the dance of images in Goya's early opening to states of spirit & mind that many of us would later come to share.

    The title *A Book of Concealments* is based, almost literally, on a Jewish mystical work, *Sifra diSeni'uta,* from which I drew the lines that open the present work as preludes & earlier arranged them with commentary in *A Big Jewish Book.* Those lines appear sporadically throughout *A Book of Concealments,* not as the mapping of a nonexistent god, but as an intimation, in both *Concealments* and *Caprichos,* of an imagined world embedded in the real one. The writing of these poems at a time of *new* wars & *new* dissimulations—a notable change since the writing of *A Book of Witness*—is another circumstance not to be ignored.

Jerome Rothenberg
Encinitas, California
January 2010

THE SLEEP OF REASON
for Clayton Eshleman

Words imprinted on a sign
by Goya   glowing
white against a surface
nearly white:
the sleep of reason
that produces monsters.
He is sitting on a chair
his head slumped
resting on his arms
or on the marble table,
pencil set aside,
his night coat open
thighs exposed.
All things that fly at night
fly past him.
Wings that brush an ear,
an ear concealed,
a memory beginning
in the house of sleep.
His is a world where owls
live in palm trees,
where a shadow in the sky
is like a magpie,
white & black are colors
only in the mind,
the cat you didn't murder
springs to life,
a whistle whirling in a cup,
gone & foregone,
a chasm bright with eyes.
There is a cave in Spain,
a fecal underworld,
where bats are swarming
among bulls,
the blackness ending in a wall

his hands rub up against,
a blind man in a painted world,
amok & monstrous
banging on a rock.

THIS WAITING GAME

A woman in a mask
is like a queen.
She gives a hand to those
who give her theirs,
the monkey faces
& the faces
of old tarts.
She trembles
& the crowd
below the stage
applauds her.
It is late.
A woman leaning on a stick
tells time. Her hands
are sensible.
Before the night
is halfway done
a stranger will assault
her bed.
This ravishment
is all that stands between
her fate & yours.
This waiting game.

A CHILD BESIEGED

A child besieged. A child
in terror sits
before her. Mothers
watching who arrive in
full length gowns,
a cloth that covers all.
My mother is my daughter,
& the other face,
the one behind,
is half a boy   disguised
& frightened unto death
of something
that has never been
but now
may change to something
palpable
a final circumstance
that only
is.

LIKE A BEGGAR

What man, his lips
heavy with hair,
assumes a young girl's look?
What moustache trembles
on that mousy face?
Why does his finger push
so deep into
his mouth   a tooth
comes loose
his moist tongue curled
to cough it up?
Who sets the table
that his elbows rest on?
& who is it who
waits behind him,
back bent,
like a beggar,
bathing at a trough?

THE LADY WITH THE FAN

The mask still there
—like shades
over her eyes—
just when the sky goes grey,
the man beside her
turns into a shadow of
himself   of all the others
who are also shadows.
Nobody speaks, except the crones
behind them, seated
on a rocky ledge,
are smiling, pointing
a sharp finger
at the lady with the fan,
the mask,
the hollow sky,
the man whose coat has come undone,
revealing air.

THE WORLD A MASQUERADE

Hats the men wear
—striped—
atop their heads
so ugly & so cruel
the murky air
won't hide them.
One averts
his eyes, the other
stares at you
with hatred
fierce enough to freeze
your blood.
A third one sits,
a lump down on the ground,
his good eye riveted
on empty space
or on the rump of someone
bending over
—man or girl—
with hat pulled tightly
over ears,
in deference to
the woman in the mask,
her gown adorned
with spanish laces.
Nadie se conoce,
Goya writes,
but all are gay
deceivers,
the world a masquerade
for those like you
who run from it   for those
like me who stay.

A SINGLE GLASS, A MONOCLE

Poor caballero,
how will you tell the world
in which the woman
dwells, her ringed hand
covering her breast,
her other bringing forth an object,
hidden, that you squint at
through a single glass,
a monocle,
while from behind
the lady with the fan
sits on a chair
& watches where you go about
the nightly work.
Too late, too lost,
somebody's boy peeks out
between your haunches.
He is the last to know
or care   pay him no mind
but pull your hat back
with your free hand,
knowing that outside the frame
the beggars lie in wait,
who steal the clothes off
any body that they find.
Love conquers all.
A wink is like a waggle.
Day is night.
The secret lies inside
your pocket,
hidden:
PAY THE PRICE
& DIE.

THE MAN WITHOUT A FACE

The man without a face
is still a man.
The words repeat themselves,
red in his throat,
the pressure of the woman's arm
against his back,
her body sagging,
legs upheld by someone
like a goblin,
sheeted, cavernous.
No mask remains.
No mouth.
No lips.
No particle of skin.
No price to pay.
No cash.
The holiday has reached
its peak.
The two who carry her away
are bundled   plunderers
engaged with time & space.
Her head is hanging
free. Between
her teeth a scream.
is taking shape.
Her hair comes loose
& floats
down to the ground.
There is no place for her
to stand, no door
to hide behind.
The sky inside the frame
is painted black,
on which she casts her eyes
but fails to see.

TANTALUS

There is a pyramid
deep in his dream
the happy fat ones
run from.
They have left the stage
forever, seen the lights
go crazy,
& can't sleep.
The man who holds a woman
on his lap, unhinged,
starts weeping.
God is on his mind
his eyes are blank
& fixed
on nothing.
He is no different from
the ones who die
for love.
His name is Tantalus
but now the tongue
is dead inside
his mouth. The stranger
must be bleeding
but they do not see
the blood, the woman's
arm obscures it.
Love & death
are foreign words.
Their mouths fall open,
partners to each other's
cravings. Take
this liquor from
its thimble.
Suck it till your lips
turn raw.
It will never

slake your thirst
& you
will slowly learn
to die from what
it leaves you.

THE COMPANY OF MEN

Those who are *real* men
stroke their knives & wait
under the rocks, their guns
at ready. Mindless
their eyes are, like the eyes
of reptiles, tight
the flesh over the bone,
the blood like snow
dyed pink. It is
the company of men
that shapes the world,
some who are friends
& others
in it for the sport.
They chew & pick their teeth.
The end of strife
unmans them. Life is death
& death
is what is lost,
retrieved,
& lost again.
Men who are *real* men
rub their skin
with death, a paste
of fat & ash.
They marvel at
the splintered tree
behind them,
the papers strewn about,
wine spilled,
the sky a blister.
They will go to war
& you, because
your time is drawing nigh,
will wait in wonder,
trembling to be born.

INTERLUDE ONE

Caught in the game called
los caprichos
I am as good as gold,
no cleaner & no worse
for wear. The thought
engorges me.
I buy eggs at half the price
paid by the others.
It brings me to a height
where few prevail,
a ledge where someone begs
for soup   a mother
or a fool.
I am a little man with hands
that swing a whip,
a fan that chills the air.
I murder those who follow
where a monkey
leads   anxious
to be understood
& loved. Their ruler
is a dupe,
their circumstances
overwhelm me.
In the night I glide between
the little shops,
the hovels of the circumcised,
the souks & casbahs.
I pretend to be a dog.
Men barter women,
not too dear
& not too stale for love.
A masquerade
is more than God
can bear,
less than what I proffer,

ending where I do,
the thought of his caprichos
on my mind,
ready to play my part.

THE POWER OF THE DEAD

See the woman
on tip toes,
fancy shoes bent back.
She turns aside.
She holds a cloth
over her cheek.
She smells the effluence of death
& with her free hand
& her fingers
probes his mouth.
The wall is black. The man
above the wall
is dangling,
rope around his neck
& wrists.
The ground is lost to him.
His feet still stretch
to touch the platform,
shoeless,
but in death
no breath is left him.
Once the moon has waned
the night grows doubly
dark. A tooth
breaks loose & trembles
in her hand.
Is it the gold she seeks
or something stronger,
the power of the dead
to change the world?
A curse. A cure.
What was the song she used to sing?
The door
is not a door
until a dead man
leaves through it
& stares out sadly, crucified
some bloody morning.   (F.G. Lorca)

THEY ARE HOT

They are hot
& what they eat
is also hot.   It is
the mouth that makes
the man, the gown
that makes the monk.
We know this hombre
by his mouth   lips
spread so far apart
it shows no teeth,
it is a dark hole leading to
a darker hole.
His gullet empties every hour,
his spoon, intact,
is hanging in the air.
One of his brothers groans
while eating,
another leans away
& laughs. The darker servant,
set against a giant
moon, is bowing,
bobbing. Light
has sprung from nowhere,
strikes the table
& the gown,
the bald man's pate.
Is it the light of reason
or of faith
that glows around them,
a switch turned on
that shows us terror
as a human face?

QUÉ SACRIFICIO!

The eye of the beholder
bulges   just in time
it knows the ugly man is ugly,
knows the sacrifice
is from the bottom up,
the young girl offered to
the troll   she turns aside
demurely
through her closed eyes
no light flows.
The others, standing guard
feel how their blood
churns, egg him on
or crack a smile
or shield their own
eyes. Each one
takes a turn.
Each has the smell of sex
keen in his mind,
the small man's legs
like claws
clamping around her.
Qué sacrificio!
The man with pebbles in his pockets,
bib tucked under chin,
prepares to snare his prize.
There is nothing in the world
more deep
than destiny   no sacrifice
like what the girl makes,
the promise of the perfect match
forgotten   hidden
in the hump,
the lump he carries
like a bundle
on his back.

THE END COMES WHEN IT DOES

The young & the old
change places
& will continuing changing
in the nick of time.
Old mothers sicken,
then they die.
The end comes
when it does   the reckoning
lost in the shadows
from which the mother beckons,
leans her head against
the daughter's arm.
A swarm of mothers now,
their voices
like electric bees,
is never far from where
the hag steps forth
poor doll with winter eyes
with one last yarn
to spin. The mothers fall down
hard, encumbered
by old baggage. They have sat
all night & pared
their toe nails to the bone
& only then gone out
to snag
their daughters.
Every mother's child is up
for sale. *The streets
of Buenos Aires drag down
many a poor soul,*
the old song says.

TIGHT STOCKINGS

Tight stockings
make a man's balls swell
they say. They play
love like a game,
place a slippered foot
on a bidet & rock around
the clock. Old women
count the days,
the hours left behind,
the thrusts made
by the perfect pelvis.
Some body with a name
like yours   steps
from his clothes,
a dream of women in
tight stockings
filling half his brain,
the other half
long gone.
A chair goes up in flames.
The man remains inside
a burning house,
the sand dissolving
in the pit.
He dreams about his own leg
stuffed into its silk,
the fit of which
is like a miracle
& heats him.
Few of them remember
what began it,
thinking
they were always there.
Now that his pants
are halfway down

he looks at them
with wonder,
thinks that they're halfway
up.

ALL WHO WILL FALL

A swarm of little birds
with heads of men
& women,
this is his dream
& yours.
The mothers in the world below
hold back a laugh   a fart
that dances in the air
between them. One is old
& holds a bone
between her fingers,
watches how a daughter
prongs the screaming
bird man, props him
on another's lap,
the spittle from his mouth
against her dress.
All who will fall,
like these,
have one commitment,
it is not to you
but to the air
they ride on.
Some are angels,
some are myopic men,
the one atop the tree
a woman known for envy,
hidden thoughts,
a fountain at her source.
Adrift or flying
backwards,
theirs is the fate of sailors.
Bind them   pluck them.
Those who have enough of dreams
wake every morning,
ready to be the slaves

of those who dream for pleasure,
naked & wounded,
eager like them
to kill.

TO SPEAK AS WHO YOU ARE

To speak as who you are,
say "I"
then streak across
the tiled floor,
little naked birds
your feathers stripped from you.
Lost, without wings
you feel the heaviness
of time, like those
who stalk you,
those who strike the air
with brooms
& banners,
signatories
to your days on earth.
Old women sneer,
young women snicker,
the door that opened onto China
fills with light,
the stubs of feathers
sting you,
in the air above them
shadow of a hawk
without a head
is looming   waiting
for the kill,
the carcass to be cast aside,
like paper,
like a poem in a dream
unread but endless.
You are the last of Goya's
birds   the fatal product
of his will,
a face without a name.

THOSE SPECKS OF DUST

The men, like cats,
savage the tender bird.
They pluck her
hard   the fact of hunger
swells their lips,
their mouths that crack
a wing, a carcass
thrust against
the bald man's chin.
Bird bares her
child breasts,
eyes rolled back
in dread of
cat men.
Grown to woman-
hood she walks
with other *pobrecitas*
prisoners
of love   the streets
windswept
like Kansas   barren
faces wrapped
to hide the vestiges
of shame, of blame
those specks of dust
the brutal guards
expunge, hands rubbing
hands in glee,
foot delicately placed before
companion foot.
She is a woman made to wear
a fool's cap,
seated, clenched hands
bound with rope,
with man's face,
body neutered,

where a crowd stares up at her,
& from a pulpit,
open book
in hand,
a little man calls forth
the causes of
her shame.

THAT WHICH WE SEE IN GOYA

A woman made to wear
a fool's cap
& to ride a mule.
The road clogged up with watchers,
men on horseback,
shadows on a glass,
an eye gone dead,
a change of fortune.
Time is running
backward.
That which we see
in Goya
comes alive. It is
the punishment men dream
who live in fear
of women,
bang their bells
in anger.
Deep inside
the mind
there is a drawing
still to do.
Here are the men
whose backs are turned
against us,
others with sticks,
with curled hair
shoulder length,
unkempt,
& eyes that travel
sideways,
ready for the kill.
Nobody can call them back.
A stadium erupts
in flames. A stand
of fathers

draws a clamp around
her neck.
The past & future
intersect. God's
word is spoken,
strands you
in a foreign clime.
A fell arrest.

INTERLUDE TWO
for Anselm Hollo

A quarter after one is when
I wake, the full night
still ahead   the times untold
in quarters where a Russian prince
rumples his sheets,
the prima donna daughters
eager to please
giving no sign of
rapture.
No one asks me in,
the door stays shut,
the morning's paper doesn't come,
it drizzles.
I try writing in a book
in which the words
are volatile
& vanish
as I write them.
I like to hear my own name
coming back to me
in steamy whispers.
Never have I been
so free of thoughts,
so empty,
that I have to bow & scrape
to suit my neighbors.
Maybe if I rush
I can maintain a foothold,
push my way
into the broken frame,
display my brutal
nature. Men & women
play caprichos.
They are writing on
a wall & I

who have no past
am waiting
for the future to go up
in lights.

AN IMAGE OF THE FALLEN WORLD

A boy's butt,
naked,
waiting for the shoe
to cut down hard,
the mother's shrunken face,
wash on the line,
a broken bowl.
The cry of pain is sexual.
The mother's cry,
the babe's,
augur the days to come.
All these construct an image
of the fallen world,
heartsick to watch it reemerge
over the ages.
The young girls sit
with chairs
atop their heads,
blank faces
out of picture books,
their bodies naked.
Again the men,
marauders,
seize the abandoned moment,
the flimsy shawls,
stare where the hairs
shine through,
the girl holes glisten.
Hot for what
they see, the world
feels free to them,
they play the game
of satisfaction.
Anger brightens
every face
& paves the way
for pleasure.

A MAN TILTS BACKWARDS

A man tilts backwards,
more from sleepiness
than lust   his eyes becalmed,
his hands that hold a book
starting to uncurl.
The hired hand
who wields a comb
is free to jam it down,
another equally
to cram a foot
into a shoe.
He is their president.
He reads & sleeps
at once.
The only paradise he knows
consists of thieves
& madmen.
Money is the key
for him   for others
only time will tell.
He finds it difficult
to dream, to read
between the lines,
evade the sound
the blade makes,
feel the pressure of
a shoe against
his foot, the evening
slowly creeping in,
the flow of words
more than the eye can take,
ready for sleep.

MEN LAUGH AT MEN

Men laugh at men
& money
while craving what
the other hides,
a bag of cash
or rocks,
the trash of too much life,
too many years,
the voices of the old men
crying *shit*
like children,
old women counting beads,
it makes no difference
if the young girl
stroking her wet leg
bothers to listen,
there are others here
who pray for her,
the mothers in their thoughts
gone up to heaven,
crones & codgers,
waiting for their lives to end,
susceptible to surgeons,
shadowed by cops
into the little rooms,
flesh mongers
ready for the coup de grace,
the steamy offers
men's eyes make
on entering,
a pocketful of dollars
buys them love,
delayed transgressions,
dirty days,
& little worth.

NO GREATER HAPPINESS

Someone of little worth
he jams a hand
into the other's mouth,
pulls at his earlocks,
while a third one
vomits dark matter,
& a fourth,
a distant cousin
maybe   curls up
on a mattress
half asleep.
He is the king of craws,
the prince of palates.
From the way his fingers
move   an image rises,
a row of bottles
brilliant in the light
shot from his eyes.
The sleepers know no greater
happiness than what
the woman with her head
bent to the ground
affords them,
crouched like monks
or toweled bathers.
Back & forth
caprichos chase caprichos,
sex & fear
what drives them,
grabs them by the scruff,
their monkey faces
open, blind,
their noses plugged
with sand,
spew drops of bile
like poison.

A DONKEY & A MONKEY

Disciples of a donkey,
do they come
to learn   attitudes
& platitudes
stamped on their reptile
minds? *That parrot,*
this carrot   (Tatehata A.)
are other signs for sure.
A donkey & a monkey
facing off   caprichos
that the monkey plunks
on *la guitarra,*
soundlessly,
the donkey following
in wonder,
strangers clapping hands
& crying *hey,*
olé.
A donkey like a monkey
reads a book,
a monkey like a donkey
listens,
He sees a pair of
donkey faces,
lines of A's across
a chalkboard,
easy aces,
donkey silhouettes
in grey,
a spunky donkey
in a coat, his muzzle
pressed against
the dead man's chest
the best he has
to show   hello,
caprichos!

IN GOYA'S WORLD

Flesh down to bone
a feeble skin
that barely covers her,
her empty mouth
pushed up against her nose,
her eyes shut tight,
the two who kneel beside her,
sister crones,
squat bodies hoisting brooms,
what do they spin
so finely?
In a corner of the room
the bodies of dead babes
are hanging,
little molls like little dolls,
the chins of children
sickly   prickly
strings attached
to fingers. Elsewhere
in Goya's world
crones suck the juice from
babes   jaws loose
& braying
ancient beings tucked in cowls,
in coils,
a basket at their feet
filled with babe's bodies.
It is too late
too late,
the bodies hang no longer,
all have fallen,
the women pass a dainty
box from hand to
hand, their fingers
dig down deep,
they slip the bones,

the little seeds,
between their lips,
into their gullets,
always still more to suck,
still always hungry.

A WITCH'S BREW

An angel crouched
as if to shit
commands the upper world.
Those gathered
smell a witch's brew,
a stew half hidden
under her white robe.
The face she wears
is not a face,
not human,
from an age before the fall,
time lost to us,
a stage where men
& animals
are one. A stranger
in dark glasses
near the mother rat
his mind like yours or mine
holds the final secret,
mothers poring over books
or praying   knobby hands
squeezed tight.
The little man over their heads
is like a bat   his legs
an ape's legs,
a prehensile big toe
sucking air
two squatting humans
at his side.
The Witch of Barahona
licks them into shape,
signals the rites of bliss
& piss
before she sets them free.

THE FALSE ACADEMY DISSOLVES

A babe
stiff as a whisker,
candy hard,
rock simple,
crying without a voice,
a sacrifice
made to the mother
rat her face
uplifted   mouth
empty as hell is,
will she not raise
the dead doll
to her lips,
become devourer
of babes?
The false academy dissolves,
its denizens amok
& crouching,
crones & codgers
in a heap,
their gums & tongues askew
teeth screwed in place,
jaws snapping,
the grandest of them
she who dominates
the pack
larger than life,
who plays *the great
deliverer.* Unbuttoned
little men would die
to suck her dugs
& lie there,
propped atop a mound
of swollen flesh,
their own desires rising,
issuing in drops

of viscous jelly,
where someone else's
wish is nobody's
command.

INTERLUDE THREE

I hold a cross
between my teeth
& suffer.
Children grow crooked.
Jesus saves
from hell. It rains
on our parade.
The gods among the dancers
trade caprichos,
not the least among them
calls out from
the curb,
you see that,
see the way my fingers
string a ring around
your throat   the way
I click & pick
the little boomers,
little bells.
The dancer falters,
finds no time
to wiggle free,
to linger. Circumcised
is circumspect,
I run the gauntlet,
hide my words
inside a cave,
a basket,
catch the shadow of a cat,
a rat,
hang by a whisker,
whistle till I fall
to earth, my face
like yours   an angel
without teeth,
her hair in flames.

THESE CLOWNS
CALLED DUENDECITOS

Screaming, streaming bubbles
from his mouth
& bunghole
little man with wings,
bat father
rides astride a cat,
a giant cat paw
at his thigh
the cat mouth
open wide, he claws
& you claw too,
the cry of something wild
shatters their ear drums,
& the crone
bends over
but her hands in fear
can't block it.
Curs look outward
with disdain   they are
another kind of people,
puckish, playful,
smiling little men
with hands the size of hams
& tender tiny feet,
these clowns called
duendecitos,
holding wooden cups
or poking fingers
soaked in wine
& piss
into their craws.
A window in a cellar
behind bars
the light pours through,
their priestly garments

rise   surprises
of the flesh
await them,
eyes stare out of eyes
uncaring
capes they drape around them,
some of these days.

NOTHING BUT THE AIR
THEY BREATHE

Sweet bliss, sweet
ignorance,
his eyes stitched tight,
the monster's
mouth hangs open,
waiting
for the spoon to find
its mark   a silver
residue against
his tongue.
The monster in the dirt
is less
a man but lies
aghast, his fingers
counting beads.
Two monsters,
padlocks on
their ears,
a scream
half formed,
their bodies
wrapped in quilts
beside a long eared
keeper   nothing
to be heard
& nothing known
or done,
a tribe of monsters
good for
nothing but
the air
they breathe,
heavy with silences
breaking
around them.

THE ONE WHO CUTS IS NAKED

No one so crude
a well-aimed scissor will not
trim the toe nail,
let the talon
slip into the dust,
the faintest shadow
of a smile
lining the creature's
lips   how happy
to be thought a man
with legs crossed
sitting, high
on cushions
sheltered by the leathern wings
of him whose face
darts snakelike
from a body
like a black hole
cut in space,
a sky & puffs of clouds
behind his pinions,
talons poking through,
unsheathed.
The one who cuts
is naked,
he is bald & brings
the other's toes
close to his face.
The sheet on which
his shadow falls
catches the fragments,
a shower of cuticles
pale as the sky,
the lonely souls
rejoicing   proud
to be spruced up,

to know the world's end
when it comes
will be their own.

A WHACKY LEVITATION

Every mother's child
can pray,
her blissful face
unlined,
who kneels before
a body with
no mouth   no trace
of eyes
with sleeves from which
two leafy branches
break   no fingers
but with arms
outstretched,
his shadow
wrapped & caped
is rising in the air,
a whacky levitation,
to which a line of sinners
prays & sobs
& others,
watching from the sky,
lie crouched,
their arms around
their legs,
the while a grim man,
riding on
an owl,
hides one hand
behind him
& the other hand
half buried
cold against
his sex.

THE WAY THE BIRD'S FOOT HOVERS

Golden birds
like golden men
prance on a platform.
What authority!
What grace!
The way the bird's foot
hovers, half
imperial
above the quaking elders,
makes us repine.
A cemetery opens.
Those who heal
are healers,
those who bind the wounds,
their minds fixed
blindly
on the task,
leave us behind.
What is told
is sold
& what is sold is solid,
soiled & spoiled.
A doctor talks in rhyme.
He writes a line to test
translation, a word
a bird repeated,
seated & tame.
A face lurks at the corner
of the platform
—a golden beak—
whose setting is *romantic,*
frantic & ecstatic,
raptured,
captured,
buried in blank spaces,
narrow places,

perilous,
the perfect getaway for
Goya's ghost.

A GAME CALLED UP & DOWN

A face so miserable
he sticks it
nose thrust forward
down his pants leg,
sniffs the hairy skin,
seduced by gruel
a cruel mother
digs into the dead man's
bowl & spoons out
slowly, fitfully.
The sight of it
makes someone
—Goya maybe—
tighten his fists
& scream
against the men who prize
their faces above all,
who sit like ancient women
at their mirrors,
preening,
while the young bloods
stare them down
or snicker,
fingers to their lips,
eyes turning blindly
skyward.
We are in a game called
up & down
A smiling man holds fire
in his hands,
his head in flames,
a giant with a horse's legs,
stripped naked,
grasps his ankles,
bears him up,
while all around them

bodies tumble,
faceless men
in pairs
over a marbled
earth.

HOSANNA, HANNAH!

Search & seize
to know
the lady is no lady
but a mask,
a dog's snout propped in place,
hiding her own.
Hosanna, Hannah!
She who used to juggle
words   conceal them
under wraps,
the shrunken bridesmaid
standing at her side,
a book in hand,
her finger pointing
to the letters
that now glow
& cover
other letters,
with a stub of pencil
set to catch
the words in flight.
The darker witnesses are those
whom Goya calls
the Filiation,
abuelos & abuelas
gawking thru steamy glasses,
a falcon's beak attached,
a swollen face
scuffing her lap,
a head thrown back
in rapture.
Theirs is the pedigree
no one will claim,
the lineage abandoned,
their inheritance
& ours   the future

squeezed thru a syringe,
a shabby heritage
ready to shine.

SWALLOW IT, YOU DOG

Squeezed thru a syringe,
so large & heavy
that the man who holds it
staggers with the weight,
the fear of men in gowns,
in robes, in vestments
the new time binding us
to Goya's apparitions.
Whose is the face behind
the veil   the dark man
still a mystery,
greater than the god is,
& another
with a pouch around
his neck, his hands clasped,
begging to be bound,
illumined by a torch
another holds,
& still another plays
with strings that move him
like a puppet.
Swallow it, you dog,
the man who wears
a white gown cries
in agony,
the fathers laughing,
waiting for the serum
to invade, to soak his bones,
his scrotum,
in a game of real men,
elders whose caprice
is victimhood.
Each is the other's dog,
each testifies
to what confounds him,
like a drone.

THE DOMINATION OF THE GOAT

A stone slab hangs
over the father,
nearly a bag of bones,
who presses, puffs
his life out
to deflect its fall.
His women cower,
helpless,
he is all that stands between
the praying mothers
& their spawn.
A feeble enterprise,
so near that other frame
no one can get to,
the domination of the goat
as master maker,
god presiding
over naked
bride & groom.
The man child
floats on air,
a hand upraised
to block her
that will touch
her smiling face,
her own hands
cup his locks,
his ears,
the ground beneath them
strewn with bobbins,
trussed birds,
cats who hunt for dregs
in earthen jars
& glare at you,
a skull pressed in the earth
absent a cross.

What trials these are
to live through,
while the goat stands
upright   striped horns
blotting out the heavens,
feet firm in place.

INTERLUDE FOUR

I dance with little men,
my trolls & fathers,
the ones who tap
their breasts
& cry "my heart"
"vacuity"
"luxation."
Their language starts to rhyme
& scatters.
In the ways I choose
no one is first
or foremost
none more engaged
than I.
I am a foil for monsters
neither Goya
nor the kings of water
can forfend.
Curs trail behind me.
witnesses to sex,
their bliss is mine,
cats' tongues,
the eyes of dogs,
my fingers
tracing lines along
her naked body.
On the silver screen
the spirit of romance
runs riot. I will be
your chronicler,
not more nor less,
your clown   at once
a subtle dancer
& a minister,
too mindful of the prize
to let it lie.

THE DAUGHTERS OF VIRTUE

Arms spread
like an eagle in flight
or a bat,
the lady
is spanish   the lady
wears a mantilla,
ribbons & combs
in her hair,
her feet half touching
the heads like balloons
she drifts over.
The heads are the heads
of old women.
They fill up with gas
& hold sway
where the lady strides
over them,
clouds at her back,
an ocean lies under her.
Who would have thought it!
A woman fucked
by a woman,
naked,
their bodies struggling,
linked to a terror
electric like sex.
The lady bright like
a butterfly
vanishes. Framed
by the night,
they tear at their throats,
at their hair
while out of the earth
a beast lunges
bear-like   a cur
with fanged teeth

& pronged claws,
every inch closer
to reach them,
screechy & grizzly,
the daughters of virtue.

BREATHLESS WITH ADORATION

She rides on horseback
& becomes
a horse. He rides
& where his face had been
a hawk's face
opens its beak wide,
the body of a man
with clawed feet,
paws that circle paws,
his own, whose legs
another's arms
have seized,
a donkey with a body
black with fur.
Limbs grasp at limbs
enwrapped,
enraptured,
brujos solemn as
a nun   breathless
with adoration.
Tiny figures overrun
a distant landscape,
those who dance,
who raise mantillas
in the sunlight.
What a show for
brutes, for voyagers
on cow paths,
empty fields & stadiums,
transformed,
transfixed,
transmogrified.
He is the muscled rider
of her dreams
& she is less a slattern
than a slut.
Ankle deep in umbra:
Buen viaje!

LIKE PALE BALLOONS

Buen viaje
out of hell,
no hope
or promise,
only the heads
of babes
like pale
balloons the wing'd
dark messenger
bears through
the night.
They fly by stealth,
escape your eyes
& guns,
only to end up
where their mama
leads the pack,
her breasts & belly
fat & naked,
thighs like stacks of
sacked potatoes.
Someone squats
beneath her rump
& someone sucks
her paps   a man
without a head,
a head turned
upside down between
a third man's
legs akimbo,
gobbles sex
like lemon curds,
a cat & an umbrella
flying by.

IN A CAT'S WORLD LIGHT IS BLACK

No easy instrument
the snake on which the cat
glides, mouth ajar,
sails through the air.
A broken devil
with black wings looks like
a hulk in flight,
sans sex, his hands
thrown back,
rump overgrown with lumps,
a naked witch
astride his lap,
his crutch a sylvan pole
a cat can sink
its claws in.
In a cat's world
light is black,
the king of cats presides   *for Mary Shelley*
over his coterie
at grave side,
proffers a coffin with a crown
plastered in place,
a dream cat soaring
toward the sky,
his haven of a home
forsaken. Up
is down.
The little towns below them
fade into the fog,
a ghost voice calling
"There it goes."
 Slowly the snake unravels
& the cat king,
riding the frozen air,
savors its body.
A generation of crazed cats,
kings of our chimneys,
after the fall.

HERE WHERE THE SPRING HAS LOST ITS VERDURE

It is the boniness of age
that brings them down,
here where the spring has lost
its verdure   this old man
with ears like wings
who wields a paint brush,
dips it in a pot of oil
& mash, will raise it to anoint
the billy goat, their courier
& king. *How light*
the sky is here,
how dark
across the page.
That couple riding on a broom
like two lost witches,
feel the stick
against their sex,
how easily it glides,
a blackhaired maiden
& a crone,
both with a sense of
desperation,
skimming the thin air.
Is the owl overhead
their mentor?
And the watchers down below,
what do they see
or do they?
They have become
so small,
a million laughs
still not enough
to make them happy.
Wet & black
they will stand guard

till morning,
better wakeful
than to be bathed in sleep,
poor souls,
& made to dream.

THE LUXURY OF PLEASURES HIDDEN

To make a babe a bellows
so that they blow it
out his ass   igniting flames,
the luxury of pleasures
hidden, Goya's monsters
even now engaged
in foul caprichos   like a fart
an article of faith,
the babes brought to the table,
not for sex
but food   for sex
and food.
An angel mother
stretches out her arms
above them, cries
into the dark,
another lugs twin babes
ready to skew,
to screw at almost
fever pitch.
A babe redeemed
becomes an ape,
sucks on his thumb,
can't bear the weight
of monkey babes
who cover the rank
ground beneath, look up
with faces peeled
like masks, reduced
to skulls.
These men are thin
but powerful
& hungry.
No one escapes from them.
They track us down
& when we fall
they rise.

SHE IS THEIR SLAVE &
SPRINGS FOR THEM

They pry the pages of a book
apart   from which
the scraggly virgin reads,
ears long & pointed,
legs around the centaur's
head, perched
on his shoulders.
She is their slave
& springs for them,
to sweep, to spin,
to ring bells,
howl, yell, fly, cook,
grease, suck, bake, blow.
The men who hold the book
are cardinals   the others
raise their heads
out of a pool of sand,
their bodies lost.
Devout profession
that ensnares them,
leads them through a night
with stars,
congeries of bodies
naked   squashed,
the foremost (prince
or princess) tilted
forward, chin propped up
by thumb
& toothless like
his good companions,
eyes wide shut,
a heavy shadow
hanging over them.
They will await
the daybreak.

In the glimmer of an eye
a particle will fall,
bird calls will sound
inside their heads
like howlers
whirling, calling forth
the names of God.

YOU WILL NOT ESCAPE

You will not escape
however much you flaunt
your innocence.
Those who thrash around you
smell your juices
while you dance, your body
wrapped in gauze,
a dress fresh as the empire,
dancer's slippers,
arms white & bare,
enticements
for the grinning
bird-men, some
with eagle feathers, others
flailing bat wings.
It is better to be lazy,
where the mother
grips the hands of strangers,
men with monkey
faces, velvet jackets
sharp italian shoes
with points. He trades
his laziness
for hers. She turns
aside, can't tell
the groom
from the duende,
sees them leap
into the air
together, buoyed
by a whirlwind.
Don't scream, stupid
someone cries
& springs at her.
There are strings that swing
between them

till she becomes
a dancing doll,
the muse of his caprichos.
pale & frail.

WHO CAN UNTIE THEM?

Pale & frail
the strings have bound her
strapped around
her waist, her ankles
where the ropes
cut in.
Tied to him
& to a winter tree,
the dream of reason
dies in her   the owl
grown to monster size
claws at her face.
Who can untie them?
Push after push
comes up against
a cabal of old men
with sticks
& whacky hats,
cockades & beavers
in hasidic black,
gay caballeros
not so gay   they clack
splayed tongues
till daybreak.
On an adjacent
block a carnival
sets out. The man
who plays the bull,
a mask like a cocoon
atop his head,
with horns,
will also play the rider.
Ghostly picadors
assail him,
ratty costumes from
a vanished time,

& prick the wormy
skin like rubber.
Faces & mouths
a Munch will resurrect,
bone china white
& without eyes.

CODA, WITH DUENDES

Duendes sound a last
hurrah   they squeeze
a bellows, scrub a dish
with greasy hands,
a whisper
in an ear bent down
to listen.
No one sees them.
Over every duende
falls the shadow
of a greater duende.
Holy moly!
Is this not a black sound,
Mister Lorca?
Pissing olive oil
I isn't what *I* seems
to be   a poor
partaker
barrel overturned,
the wine *I* swigs
gone rancid.
There is now an end
to everything.
What is flesh
they suck no more,
they drive the foul caprichos
out of sight.
Caprichos, Goya, Lorca,
all my duendes,
locked into a cage
at dawn, evading
sleep & dreams,
those whom they leave
behind them, fathers
raising arms
to heaven,

screaming through
their empty
mouths   like caverns
black holes
where all light
is lost.
Now is the time.

POSTLUDE: EIGHT POEMS IN BLACK, AFTER GOYA

two women watch
a man   his hand
under his cloak
or in his pants   the act
that causes one
to grin, the other
wisely looking on
as in a dream

*

a procession of
old whores & madams
toothless
bearing fardels
& a gallant
from a former time
lined up along the base
of a grey mountain
holy crones
& well-laced fathers
of the inquisition

*

A PILGRIMAGE FOR SAN ISIDRO

who but the dead
can scream so
with their eyes rolled back
their mouths
like black holes
whom a blind man leads
strikes a guitar
& to his left

two men in black
two women in half-white
without a face

*

Saturn
devouring his sons
whites of his eyes
as brilliant as
the red blood flowing
from the severed
neck
blood on his hands
his penis hot
& throbbing

*

man fighting man
with cudgels
drawing blood
a stream of red
across his face
& sinking
ever deeper
into the mud

*

a poor dog
hidden in the brown
& yellow mud
that could be clouds
—*the way they suffer
without sound*—

*

THE WITCHES SABBATH (1)

Satan as a great
goat   black
& holding court
before a ring
of men & women,
too deformed
from watching
the small figure
crouching
covered with
white shroud,
& at the edge
a young boy,
almost cut
from sight
the only
gentle soul,
whose screaming
mother hollers
at the assembled
crones

*

THE WITCHES SABBATH (2)

red more brilliant
than her eyes,
the blanket set across
her mouth,
poor doll & witch,
& yet the eyes
are turning backwards
in her head,
the one who flies with her,
a rock between

his teeth, a tongue
made stone,
the yellow wind
spiking his hair,
who has no choice
but points a finger
at a hill in space,
a city on a hill,
that vanishes.
Nothing has changed
since then,
try as we will,
nor will it please you,
friend & father,
the ragged soldiers
aiming guns,
the line of pilgrims,
barely seen,
circling the lonely fell,
the old witch
like a sibyl
arisen from your dream
driven to tell it all.

Finished: 22.vi.08

A BOOK OF CONCEALMENTS

The Small Face is "You" and the Shekinah is "I"

FOUR PRELUDES

(1)

a skull

—

the crystal dew inside it

—

a skin of air

—

a wool beard

—

his force is written on his forehead

—

the eye stays open

—

whose nostrils breathe life
to the world below

(2)

pepper & grain

——

outside the circle

——

two threads, one side
in red
one side in black

——

their backs were full of eyes

——

three heads included
in a single head

——

a daughter nourished
by a son

——

"I have loved you"

(3)

"your eyes"
"your eye"

———

from white to black
to green

———

the hairy lord

———

on one stone
seven eyes

———

the whiteness of the skull

———

in the Book of Concealment

(4)

my head filled with dew

——

seven runners
come forth
they lean toward the left side

——

there is no left eye

——

fire & smoke
from the nostrils,
two tears from the eyes

——

everything is concealed

——

white or pink

——

"she eats & wipes her mouth"

A BASER DEATH

A man walks
where a flower
grows
& picks it
with his teeth.
For days it dangles
from his lips,
a face without
a skull,
a twisted wire.
A hand slides under his shirt.
Candidly
the man talks
to the wind.
We are a malcontent
& thoughtless
people. Now we learn
to freeze,
who once had cast away the sun
& would not bend.
A man who trades a flower
for a tongue
will learn to speak in
rhymes. His breath
will not outlast
his smile
& he will die
a baser death
than those he thwarts.

RIGHTING AN ANCIENT WRONG

The way her knee swells
& she feels it
swelling & it turns into
a babe's head.
No one has a countenance
more rich
& no one has a mouth
that opens wider,
lets a sound like
dreaming come into
the room in which
they wait. So practical
it is to ride on air
to be a man or woman
growing wings
righting an ancient wrong
or casting a new spell
to trap the dead.
A chemistry
without a cause
theirs is a metamorphosis
for two. Soon
they switch their sex
like light bulbs,
practice with their eyes
& tongues, the work
of perfect strangers.
In her mouth his finger
finds a pearl
the object of his search
& bags it.
Bulbous are her cheeks
like melons   singular
her inclinations.
Cream runs from her nipples
turns into a powder

cotton candy   papa's beard
sweet as your own.
She will not let you ever
press her down
but cries for baubles
in her pensive way.
She is ready for snow
now that it's over.

AN ACT OF POETRY

Muses masturbate
into the wind
like sacred dolls
or phantoms.
In the first chapter of
a nun's life
time seems lost,
the taste of bread
is somehow
made a curse,
there is no place reserved
for pleasure.
Twenty men march past
like twenty angels.
Women raised up to heaven
on thin heels
are watching, waiting.
In the space between them
others squat   small mothers
nearly mexican
& reach a hand to touch
the feet of strangers.
Is it the Paris air
that tints them,
makes of their silent words
a kind of opera?
Sex & hunger
make the world go round,
amigo. Power
drives the mind.
She in whose bed you lie
rises to greet you.
It is an act of
poetry these two
commit, never
too often.

LARGER THAN LIFE

The image & the word
over your bed
hang crucified.
The rain fades over Europe.
Men & angels
dance before the sun,
a dead snake
dangles
from a tree,
the babe
with glaring eyes
stamps on a half chewed
apple. Happy days!
The radio is playing
songs our mothers sang,
leaving their minds
at rest.
The boy beside her bed
waits for her hand
to rest in his,
her lips to form the words
once muted
now erupting in a sigh.
The monitors who tell the time
signal time's ending,
no one alive or dead
to witness, no one
ready to ascend the wall
to scrub the image of
the god until it
vanishes but leaves
a stain behind
a kind of harbinger
larger than life.

LET IT BE ICE

Let it be
ice. Let ice
be the measure
of dying.
Let time
stand still &
be done.
In the wink of an eye
it is summer. The man
with his house on his back
rushes by. It is long
past our caring.
Let air mix with
air. Let those
who are dry
try water. Those
who are blind
find the sun. They are dear
to your heart.
They draw nigh.
The sun & the moon dance
& blow trumpets.
Let the earth hide
their blood, let a place
be found for
their cry. In the night
men go fishing for stars,
not a god but a babe
wields the trident.
Cables lie covered with
smut. Light erupts
on a screen. What you see
is your face   & the face
that you see, old
& blind,
is a face from
your dreams.

A LONG ANNULMENT

The cliffs of architecture
like palisades   at night
the stars in windows,
you in Tennessee
or in the heart
of Texas, someone
waiting for her train
to start, a pistol hidden
in her purse,
A Life Apart
will be the title of
your book   for which
a sinister beginning
& no end.
The curtains pull aside,
the fingers bend.
Friends make a final pitch.
To be a stranger
in a strange land
takes her breath away.
The neighborhood is somewhere
they have never lived,
therefore the streets are
vacant, strewn
with obstacles to memory,
a skewed perspective.
Better for the mind
to empty out
in dreams,
the way a body
falls, thrown
from a passing train,
forsaken.
They hold a plate
between them, on its rim
a graven message:
GOD IS PAIN.

There is a long annulment,
waiting for the light
to gather.
Then it breaks.

MARRANO NIGHTS

Marrano nights,
the Jew beside the Moor
in distant Spain.
The prince
at war with God
prays to a stone.
The scripture is a faded page.
It is the small face
staring back at him
in anger:
a book he burns
& reads
deep in its ashes
words
gone from his memory
of words.
Or is it Spinoza's
rage   the lie of God
lodged in his craw
engorging the world with
its grandeur?
A man not liked but loved,
he thinks the beautiful
is beautiful,
the facts of rotting life
kept far from him.
He beats his breast.
He bites his fingers.
He has lived too much
in the sun
& when it brings him down
the friends surround
his corpse,
they move him out of view,
the weight of gravity
too great to bear.

THEIR COMMON FATE

Little cars
in motion
where the table
slants, the wheels
leave marks
too rapid for your eye
to register.
It is their common
fate, by which
the human
& divine
fall in a single heap.
Allotments.
Shut.
The neighbors cross the boulevard
in pairs.
The door adjacent to
our thoughts   shut also.
Therefore they shift
their legs between
short bursts,
the cadence of a march,
old world, old-
fashioned melodies
unheard. A single hand
can sweep the board.
A single eye can glimpse
a shadow of the cosmos
through a pin hole.
Men & horses
dive into the sea
from which a friend
emerges   dead & cold
no more to wrest his portion,
rhymes & measures,
from your heart.
No more to shore you up.

A CITY WITHOUT PEOPLE

A city without people
is still a city.
The visitors who left
their footprints
on its streets
cannot be counted.
The dead are safe from death.
Your breath is in your lover's
throat   a skull
left sightless,
without heed or hope.
The last one down the hill
is still a stranger.
A heavy body. Red.
Red images & set in circles.
In the streets the people
are no more
than petals. Still
they gather,
taking photos of
the hapless dead.
Never will you shut
the jets in time. Your hands will not
fend off the pressures
of the splintered wall,
the pediments,
a building like a life
reduced to ashes.
The air has grown destructive,
finds a way
to bind you,
fat & swollen,
an old angel with
flayed wings
The searchers in the night
drift past you.

You will walk among them,
will give them solace,
only in your dreams.

New York City
28.ix.01

THERE IS A PRICE WE WILL NOT PAY

What the woman gives
is red. Her eyes,
the long ends of her fingers
red   the more
she stares at you
& makes you
feel the pressure of her thoughts
clashing with yours.
You are the one who signals her.
A child hides in your beard,
pretend you do not
see him, let the mother
take him back.
There is a price we will not
pay, a price the size
of Texas.
It is the fence behind which someone
plants his garden
all in red.
He or she is whom we mean
& either one
is pensive, waiting
in the corner of
your eye, the crystal
dew inside it,
then staring back at you
with mindless love.

A STEADY HAND

Not to miss life
the tall man garners
what he can,
he makes a star between his thumb
& pointer
crying for a fish.
The fathers go in search of
sticks & stones,
a day they mark by
little accidents,
a sharp turn in the road,
a bridge to nowhere.
Torn by love,
or was it sex
or was it what
he thought
it was, he shows
a steady hand
while driving,
stiffens
his resolve to reach
the outer shore.
There he can sit & cry,
despise his hands
because his fingers
smell of cunt
& semen,
what the body
can't abide or nurture
but in an outrage
casts away.

A MAN IN LOVE WITH DEATH

A man in love with death
is still a man.
He sees his hands bleed
with another's cankers, sees
the blood cold in his eye,
a rosy episode
smeared over walls & door.
The others enter through it,
sit beside him.
What does he hear?
Where does a life
begin & end?
How fast? How far?
Who but the dead
can claim an end
to numbers?
In his head he learns
to count them   with his hands
they are more real
than right.
Deceit of numbers
raising questions in the mind
that's helpless
& of doors that will not
shut   the others
waiting for a door to shut
behind them   for his voice
to be a voice
that speaks for them,
one of the lonely
dead.

A DOUBLE SCHISM

There is a pope
who waits for you,
a pope who sits on cushions,
paints his fingernails
a shade of red
so much like blood
it scares the dead away.
The men who stare at
their own faces
on the screen,
who write on air,
declare
his holiness.
By night the father
breaks apart,
halfway inside the window
cut in two.
He is four fathers
now, his eyes
awash with tears,
with bells that sound off
in his skull
A double schism
links to
double happiness.
The four who are
our fathers
call themselves
the pope.
They name their brides
America & point
their tongues
at heaven.
They are everything
his mother
wanted   ministers
of grace.

A trickle down his leg
is sign of rapture.
Two plus two is five.
The fathers without
issue are the lords
of those who do.

THE DRAUGHT OF VIOLENCE

The strut of fabled men
like women
leaves the gun uncocked,
the crown unkempt.
A glow around
the pubis   see the feathers
shine. Here sits
an apparatus
& beside it
boys flit by like bats.
The door into her bosom
closes   opens
letting in a puff
of smoke, *the draught*
of violence
that draws extinction in.
A wheel inside a wheel
spins feebly   dirt
that clogs its spokes
& turns into a mud
the mind of man
can't fathom.
Goons make love
in graves   the water
seeps between their toes
& forms
a second element.
Sky is a third.
The man who slit
the pilot's throat   not like
a man he is
but like the girl
who drove a spike
into her lover's heart
to suit their god.

THE FATAL ELEMENT

The room in which the man
is sleeping
splinters   halfway
through his dream
he feels a flow
of images escaping
from his eyes
imploding coating
bed & floor
with colors like a show
of lights
in space, a spectrum
half unseen,
unsought.
The fatal element is fire.
See, above our heads,
the wall of heat
no flesh can stand against,
the horrible in every
particle of air.
The age of fire beckons.
Times become what times
have been before.
The beggar in his tunnel
can't break free,
legs bound,
a rag against
his mouth, the fire
overwhelming
what was flesh
& bone.
The father strikes
a light   the son,
hand in his shirt,
can only
strike a pose.
They leave no clue behind.
Nowhere to run.

THE COST OF WHAT HE WANTS

This house was left
for strangers.
In the fractured space
under a lamp post,
how a little man
might walk & take
the measure,
nightly,
where his arms
hang down.
The cost of what he wants
escapes him,
he can not assess
the time.
Is there a strategy in this,
a plan that puts him
on a train,
a train that moves across
parched fields,
his world
more like a desert every day,
the worst of it
when he wakes up
& doesn't know
the room in which
he fell asleep,
in which he finds you
by his side?
The company of schemers,
once in place,
empties his coffers.
The caravans are on the go,
bespangled,
speckled,
ready to leave
hearth & home
behind.

Predictability
trips up the nomad.
He is a man
with meager resources
& stripped of hope.

THE TIMES ARE NEVER RIGHT

Warm days hanging
over San Diego,
where streets
slide into murky
canyons. What
is this but
home & what
is home
but a misnomer?
Pisces has shifted
into Aries.
Aggravated
bumps shadowing
the server's
arms are no
concern to anyone
yet called to our
attention show
a strain, a fearsomeness
hard to conceal.
The times are never right.
A skin of air is over
everything. The sun
flows like a liquid,
all the universe we see
has never happened.
There is no truth to time
except for birthdays.
In a city under siege
a ceremony
gathers, scattering
the birds.
We live forever
in the instant,
in the house we share.
A groom & bride

are figures,
smaller than a thumb
& little reckoning
how short
the passage between
death & life.

20.iii.02
for Diane's birthday

NO ONE IS LEFT TO BLAME

Nowhere to run
tomorrow, darker than
the night before,
how can a soul find comfort?
No one is left to blame.
A glass ring.
Images beyond suspicion.
What you wished
to bring about,
the opening of many doors,
comes into question.
Throwing caution
to the winds
the little band
is playing
bright cacophonies.
The sound the trumpet makes
rattles the tables.
Men & women stumble
on the way to church,
deflecting sleep,
interpreting the past
as though alive.
The reckless
reveries of priests
have little worth.
They beckon
& the screaming
father falls,
his mouth
extruding birds
that shatter windows
in the worlds
below.

THE MYSTERY OF EVIL
for Oda Makoto

The mystery of evil
rests in God,
no less in terror.   [*gematria* = 42]
Fathers who shun the world
cry scandal
where they spawn,
eyes dark as dungeons,
a wool beard
on every face.
Men grow transparent
in their rages,
oblivious the more
they claw with
longing
at each other's flesh.
The mystery of terror
rests in God,
no less in evil.
Poems are written
to the dead,
the ones
who do not speak nor share
a common language.
In the air of caves
a figure like a god
lies broken.
His glasses tumble to the ground.
His breath smells sweet to everybody.
Fools find places
where they track the stalkers,
legs that cross a line,
a line that dwindles to a point,
a point that shatters.
Stars collide.
The words of poems
go up in smoke.

Mothers brandish babes
like weapons.
There is no
boundary dividing
life from art.

A TOWN WITHOUT A NAME

for Michael Palmer

A town without a name
is still a town.
The men who ply their wares
head out one morning,
never to turn back.
The child who sleeps above us,
tongue gone numb,
gathers his coat around him
& debarks.
A gang of thieves finds refuge.
Banners flying,
marchers brave the storm.
With table set
chairs empty
the dead who suffer hunger
search for meat
in sabbath splendor.
Gardens blossom where a hand
digs deep   the rows
of laborers,
small men forgotten
like the names of towns,
bend with the wind.
Bright words like *bella*
grace their dreams,
their days degraded by
inane *lavoro.*
Theirs are forbidden thoughts.
A miracle from heaven,
long awaited,
does not come to them,
though peace
once sought,
is nearly there.
To make his point

the gangster
puts a gun against
the father's ear,
then pulls away,
stunned by the silence
that the act provokes.

THE REST IS COMMENTARY

A house to rent the admiral
the admiral is dead in,
one who tells you   I will sell
at cost   or tells you
there is nothing left
for anyone to sell
or buy. The message
someone left for you
loses its color.
(This only matters
when it does,
the rest is commentary.)
The way to settle matters,
truth to tell,
is to avoid engagement
& stick clear of snags.
Living in a state of sin
behooves us. Facts
are only facts,
while anything imagined
is an image of
the truth   scarcely
worth the thought
the mind affords it.
Brush your epaulettes until   DIRECTIONS
the gold shines through,
then prance with it.
Move fast from room to room
while making room
for prancing.
(The time of kings comes back.)
(We welcome progress.)
The fathers thrive on repetitions,
lock their doors,
& pay a price for sunlight.
One who takes

the name of hero, spied
in women's clothes,
has no more hopes
for peace, but aims
a bullet down his throat
& floats away,
his glory weeping.

HECTOR THE HERO[1]

His glory weeping
he bestows a kiss
on those he serves.
Hector the hero,
dressed to kill,
a metal guard between his teeth,
knows what he wants
but can't achieve it.
He is higher by a head
than those who taunt him,
running with a greyhound's stride
past banks & braes.
His force is written on his forehead.
Someone upsets the cart
& someone else
climbs up the down,
holds vowels in his cheeks
& flourishes.
The air is full of whispers,
legends of the canny
Scots who have
no home but home,
who huddle in
a cave of gold
& crow like slaughterers.
Hindin hiehin
hundin hohin
hindin hiehin
hihin hehin
hindin hiehin
hundin hohin
hindin hehin
hiehin hindin.
The ear lies flat against
the ground   the mind
filters the voices,

leads the charge
into some gay caledonia,
licked by the sea.

[1] Hector Macdonald, a crofter's son, began his military career as a private in the British army & later became a Major General. Fought in the Afghan war & both Boer wars, & distinguished himself when he saved the British army from total destruction at the Battle of Omdurman. Accused of being a homosexual he committed suicide in 1903. His life is celebrated in a Scottish song, *Hector the Hero*.

A STEAMY PARADISE

The eye stays open,
hot as sky
a mylar covering
over their heads,
a steamy paradise.
Who knows what road to take?
A coin reflected in a glass of water
shines. Small men
start on a summer journey,
puffed eyes peering,
dressed up to beat the band,
pale voyagers.
A star called wormwood
is no star   no balm's
in Gilead
no feet that walk on fire
trust its heat.
The strangers on the beach
cry out   pull back
& feel the sand
cold on their toes.
The name of one is Dr. Moto.
He is the beau of Carla,
daughter of the duke,
& beds her.
squawling,
caught under his net.
They follow
where the footprints lead,
down to the pan yards.
Poetry is not their *sprach,*
no more is outrage.
In a froth or frenzy
someone breaks
into the vault in which
a babe, his eyes
on fire like a doll's,
lies slain.

THE POSSIBILITY OF METAPHOR

Time comes to a stop. The fan
beats over their heads,
pukk-pukk,
& light breaks through the window
in short bursts.
We live inside a novel.
We are friends
no longer, but the journey,
once delayed,
is ever closer, opens
like a deck of cards,
a map connecting distances,
a poster with a face
& little words
extending in a line
along its sides.
The possibility of metaphor
disturbs him.
Doors slam shut.
He is nobody's fool
but runs beside
the men with guns
cocked for the final
shootout. Mocked
by some he takes you
for a comrade,
turns himself
into a raging bull,
The throngs who rise
against him
dwindle.
Hand in hand
the dead walk in a line,
hoping against hope,
like children.

It is enough. It
is enough.
It doesn't last.
The false commanders
lead the charge.
The story, started
in a dream,
is winding down.

A SIMPLE HEART

Each day, another death,
their little world
shuts down,
the big deaths fill the earth.
The time is never
right, the long & short of it
converge,
diverge.
A simple heart
shines from the breast
of strangers.
Everyone comes clattering,
climbs steps,
the more they rise
the more the just man
falls. Unsung
he is the last among the least,
their brother.
From his hump
he brings forth songs
but doesn't sing
himself.
He is the fitful mourner,
you. A face
without a man
he keeps his thoughts
from God.
His doubts run deep.
The dew drips
from his fingers,
on the perch above him
sits his secret
angel   mad
with stars for eyes
& mindless,
whose nostrils breathe life
to the world below.

CONCEALMENT AS A CRIME

The killer puts his tools aside,
confronts the glass,
his eyes stare at his eyes,
fingers reach out to fingers.
Concealment as a crime.
The more they track it down
the less they find,
eager to stay free
not carefree.
There is no end to rancor
but the few who live,
the frail survivors,
walk among the stones
& do not squawk
or squeak
their *final heartbreak.*
The killer signaling
a call to war.
In his voice a cry
lies hidden,
lost,
the final refuge of
the scoundrel,
of the poet who has sold
his poems.
The killer walks beside you,
hides his face,
the night descending
like a veil,
a kerchief set against
the moon.
A pipe falls from a sailor's
mouth. The friend
rides his Wisconsin horse,
he stops before a wall,
a gypsy wedding
in a world he doesn't know.

Forgive us.
We are strangers.
We have strayed into your houses,
lacking all cause.

IN A TIME OF WAR

Lacking all cause
they do what they have done
before   unwitting
mercenaries for the empire
men from little towns
south of your own,
dispensers of the laws of war.
Among crushed hats,
a crushed sun,
turning, witless,
fingering the hairs that grow
over their shallow faces,
theirs is a rare beginning,
a common end.
The streets of dinkytown
fail to contain
strangers who gasp for air
& drown   another day
when millions inundate
these squares
no room is left for loiterers.
A dark explosion slams
a distant world
hidden in ours,
a world where time
doesn't exist,
where those who fall behind
find their lost lives
restored unmarked
& innocent
with no attachment to the real,
no room for terror
in a time of war,
where they are far from
pain or pleasure,
further away than light

where *no* light is
nor darkness,
like the body's entry
into nothing,
nowhere,
larger than life or death.

OCEANSIDE PIER:
AMONG THE FISHERS

The line, more tangled than
the fishing lines at Oceanside,
hangs from a hundred different mouths,
coronas colored in a hundred ways
each one around a brilliant
orifice, bright droplets
white & yellow,
yellow,
red,
the red of circles,
a debris of spirit that the mind
can shape as words,
as sounds more true than words are,
waiting on a pier
above the mackerel-crowded seas,
to hear, to know, to celebrate,
to walk among the fishers,
lines of men & women
phantom residents
of phantom towns,
who fish by day,
go forth at night
into a world inhabited
by dolls,
a mannikin romance,
a gaffer wedging mussels from
black columns,
hearing voices
from below the earth
of animals,
the worlds we haven't seen
more real
than those we have.

THE SORRY MYSTICS
Little Infinite Poem

Infinity intrudes,
posits a world where everything,
repeated endlessly,
is possible.
A world caught in a mirror
too vast to be contained.
Infinities of mirrors.
The ones who see it
falter, their hands
break the glass.
They are the sorry mystics,
misfits from
the middle states,
we spy them
on a distant planet,
lost from time.
Another world contains them,
world on world,
another grain of sand,
each grain a world.
Another town to walk through,
hand in hand.
Another one like you
to be there   always
whom you will not know
but she will write her name
on stones.
Out of the earth
a farmer will dislodge
great stones
like gods
a paradise of stones.
Another earth
is theirs   who claim
a signature

in stone, a number
greater than
infinity, mapping
a mindless world.

THE SHAPE OF VULPINES

Three heads included
in a single head
the maskers take the shape
of vulpines, skulking
in the thicket,
cunning as a fox,
a badger
sly, conniving
everything you'd strive to be,
to feed your sense
of vital being.
Men besmear a bulkhead,
lay the daub on thick
& nearly perish.
Cuticle & scarfskin
mark the spot.
A finger growing from a finger.
Women imbricate
& suppurate,
their bodies
smirch a derm,
a tegument
of many colors.
White & black
& green
the maskers perch,
miraculous,
the daylight can't conceal
the darkness lurking
in the stone,
the surge reduced,
the fire dying back.

ANOTHER DAY

With little bars of soap
another day becomes
another day.
A phantom army waits
your pleasure,
little dolls go
belly up
& burst,
the end of time
is endless.
Who but "you"
& someone else
whose name
is "I"
can find the passage,
babble till your tongues
turn blue,
take turns at sex?
She is a princess,
fresh as soap
she meets you at the *gare,*
French dolls like ghosts
step forth at midday.
Everyone is *sportif*
geared for speed
never to turn a shoulder,
to name a game for love.
Their aim is circular,
it follows where you lead them,
down a secret path,
into a basement
shadowed by
your childhood dream,
a lurking hole,
then up the backstairs
lost to sleep,
concealments of a borrowed life
outside the circle.

WHAT BELIEVERS SEE

The barkers stand
on the embarcadero,
black shirts
almost white from
sunlight, almost
buried in your mind,
blind in the day
but in the night
like true believers
seeing
what believers
see   the comedy of god
cloaked as a babe
the clucking of the lucky rich
among the luckless,
clocks & death their password.
Nothing gained
is nothing ventured.
Nothing cooked is nothing raw.
Marrano nights are
christian days.
Life has no chance
where white is black,
hot cold.
How warm it gets,   *for Robert Duncan,* Passages 13
a hand in which a coin
burns   like a foot
in bronze, its underside
the purling covers.
A plash upsets the earth,
it loosens,
smells arise a jump away
from where it lands.
First it is old
& later it is new.
Now is the fire passage
named 13.

IN THE DARK DANCE, SIGHTLESS

A blind man's feast day
opens to a german
throng   midwinter doings
that a friend reports,
the taste of *speck*
in slices,
colors that the eye
can't see, the tongue
becomes the instrument
of sight. Insidious
a fire licks
the sleeper's cheek,
beneath his pale moustaches
something like a lip
curls upward, sky
at morning has the color
of a dead fish.
Bricabrac occasions,
memories,
a dish to set before
the kings of slumber.
In the dark dance,
sightless,
they are tearing at a bone,
their jaws like bears'
jaws   cavernous
their fingers dripping
porridge, clawing
at each other's nipples,
keepers of a dream.
The blind man sees
no flame or smoke
but knows it all
by tasting:
snort snort
berries
sniff sniff
mush.

THOSE WHO PREVARICATE
ARE LIARS

Those who prevaricate
are liars,
quacks & politicians,
dealing out a deck of cards,
easy with aces
loose & fast
like conjurers
grifters with a gift
for fiction,
stalkers with forked tongues,
trothless, tartuffish,
men who play at possum,
who cry wolf,
blow hot & cold,
with fingers that brush up against
a lady's nape,
negation only known
through language
lying as the truly human trait,
a hand,
five fingers,
twisting flowers
in her hair,
her face turned sharply,
smiles that burn
like knives,
a judas kiss delivered
crooked
in the halflight
man to man,
a daughter nourished
by a son,
the time suspended
until the time arrives
to break the spell.

CONCEALED IN WORDS, UNOPENED
First Version

Like a twisted sound,
a round of nadas,
solitary Dada cloud
pinned to its cardboard
the Popes of Dada
with us   witnesses
to what can't be revealed,
concealed in words,
unopened,
little cubicles of thought
contorted   skewed   imperfect
cockeyed
speakers of a twisted tongue,
who change direction
like a quirk of fate,
of circumstance,
a whiff of lemon from a twisted peel.
The rest is gradual,
a turning to the left   another
to the right,
rekindled,
then the frame flies open,
sounds of those called
dada fathers,
swinging in a ring around
a triple helix,
strings of stippled light,
fortissimo
the band plays *rubadubdub*
dub in skip step.
Rescued from time,
their backs are full of eyes,
each dancer
crammed into a corner,
jerking,
where everything is bent
or spent.

CONCEALED IN WORDS, UNOPENED
Second Version

Like a twisted sound,
a round of nadas,
a solitary Dada cloud
pinned to its cardboard
the Popes of Dada
with us   witnesses
to what can't be revealed,
concealed in words,
unopened,
little cubicles of thought
contorted   biased   warped
imperfect
speakers of a twisted tongue,
who change direction
like a twist of fate,
of circumstance,
the smell of lemon from a twisted peel
tomorrow or today,
a quirky twist.
The rest is gradual,
makes of its curvature
a rightness,
more than his twisted back
can bear.
The name they give him
he will wear
written across his forehead,
curving to right & left
over his temples:
Prince of Lies
& Turncoat
the hairy lord.
Whoever twists is called
the Twister   whirls & twirls
is never seen in silhouette

but topsy-turvy.
falling thru a hole in space
he lands
on his own body,
dances where the world
turns crooked.
Cockeyed world,
spent god.

A CLEAR ASTONISHMENT

War waiting in
the gateway
to the hive—
a clear astonishment
affronts the fallen
comrade   darker
than the bowel energies,
unleashed, the pit
also unleashed
& emptied.
We have traveled far,
only to end up
here, to feel
the winter sun
struggling to light
our faces   nothing
still left to see,
enlightenment as distant
as the stars.
To take a walk
in wartime
is again to know
the swarm, the pulsing
of a throng
always in expectation,
caught in a war
none of them
share in. *Spare me*
entreats the fitful soldier
hidden behind
his face.
The beekeeper
advances,
fire & smoke
pour from his nostrils,
two tears from
his eyes.

The reckoning
is ever certain,
never more near
than now.

LIKE GOD ATOP A TOWER

He is the hidden one,
the prince concealed in water,
man who speaks without
a pronoun to his name.
The *eye* is cruel, the other *I*
lies buried in his words,
a confluence beyond translation.
In the way the son comes forth,
caught in the sun's light,
the whiteness of the skull
more white than fire,
he is the last romantic, sits
like God atop a tower,
the perfect dog.
They who don't speak his name
grow frantic   turn a corner
will not stop
until the light imperils them
with revelation.
The days go white
with aftershocks
& black with clouds.
Mind makes way for spirit,
a ghost without a chance
to come out clean
& half a mind
to keep it down
& dirty.
Theirs is the circumstance
denied   first person singular
at bottom of our speech.
The man who writes
can do it   steel his thoughts
against the particle
cruel as the eye of him
who writes it.

A DEEP ROMANTIC CHASM
for Michael McClure

A deep romantic chasm
beckons him   it leaves no time
to hide from light
in spite of circumstances,
& the way the street
flows like a stream
from no source,
nowhere.   *This season*
with its birds
newly arrived,
the first one on a fence,
mortal as you,
a harbinger of days to come.
Another word,
a false return,
the spoken still unspoken
carries us off.
The cavern of the universe
widens each morning.
My head fills up with dew,
the father writes,
having no home but where
his shadow leads him.
In greasy shirtsleeves, heavy
lids, blotched faces,
the men pursue
a trail of tears,
unbuttoned   captive
to a dream,
a starless galaxy,
the deeper sky
a field of images
measureless & mindless,
absent their god.

THE UNIVERSE AS PRETEXT
FOR THEIR WRITING

What is hidden
hides the rest
in turn   the universe
as pretext for
their writing,
shows the alphabet
in colors,
something to be written on,
then lost.
Strapped in their seats
the passengers launch into space
like children,
half awake.
They count the time
that's left
& hide.
The metaphysics of the poem
will drive us crazy.
White or pink
their faces shine above
the portal.
Separated by a cranny
others   more aware
stare down at us
We have no way
to talk together,
mirror neurons that respond
only to themselves
& not to others.
A place to stand
deep in the speaker's mind
determines speech.
The plan is self-erasing
if we wait it out,
not one of us the worse.

for wear,
but pleased to know
the world will end
when we do.

THE PLACE CALLED ALMA

There is no left eye
but the right
sees backwards,
reaches to the place
called *alma,*
where the heart's concealed.
Abrasions mark a face
too delicate,
open to the taunts of boys
& guardians.
Her foot taps on the floor
before him.
Lost in his thoughts
he knows no word for it
or otherwise.
A heavy body.
Colors.
Of a loss in space.
An invitation to the dance
unnerves him.
"Your eyes."
"Your eye."
A dying fall
long gone   a message
left behind,
its letters throbbing
on his keyboard.
Bathed in light,
a world ends,
life by life,
it finds its own
concealment,
swinging toward
that dark time,
where the sun is eaten,
never to be reborn.

NOW THAT HER TURN COMES

She eats & wipes
her mouth,
& those who watch her
fail to see the shadows
that conceal her eyes,
The screen blurs,
the message she would send
stuck in her throat.
Between her fingers
she can feel
the stirrings of a heart,
false weather,
shocks against her skin.
On one stone
seven eyes—
what else is left
to say   what makes
a murderer
the last romantic?
Lurching down a corridor
under a town
the man who would escape
drops to his knees.
A fatal hole
with people
locked inside it,
reaching for the light.
No prayer
so easily expendable,
no eyes to see.
They are deceived
by peace
but know the century
once under way
returns them
to a broken world.

Now that her turn comes
she can only bend
& smile.

A MAN WITH A HOLE IN HIS EYE

Seven runners
come forth,
they lean toward the left side.
The far edge of the earth
tilts inward,
connections break loose,
spring comes late.
The man with a hole in his eye
sees anew. A sphinx
fingers a sphincter,
she extrudes
false colors. The night
once was pink,
it is now
black & white.
Nerval in a corner
spitting his death out,
a substance
first dreamed,
then stuck under
his tongue.
The war goes on forever
Cities drown.
The death of God
is credible,
a blank spot
in the center of
his vision,
something he takes
for granted
as his cat takes life.
This is the price
of second sight—
a light under a bushel,
buried
as blinding as day.

THERE IS NO PROOF OF ANYTHING

Blinding as day
the light's no sooner
seen than hidden,
turtle doves above
like lamps, like lights
all over
the night sky,
different from
that other sky
they witnessed,
black & clear
but starless.
There is no proof
of anything
beyond this thought,
no time to talk,
to make a wish come true
or stop the progress
of that deeper night
that calls us.
Those with a love of death
stand fast.
They wear the masks of men
eager to conceal
their frailties,
their human nature.
Someone who knows your name
awaits you,
you would think,
but searching through that sky,
above those birds,
there is no terminus,
no end to time
& no beginning.
That much has been revealed.
The rest is commentary,

fit for a thrall
& barely
numbering our days.

THE WORLDS WE KNOW

Alone & nowhere
more alone
he waits for morning,
walks to the balcony
& stares.
A squad of runners
circles a distant hill,
the disappearing shadow
fading from the rock
like water
in a red hot sun.
The worlds we know
are virtual,
dead
at the entry.
The pleasure when it comes
makes up for all,
then disappears
in turn. The man
who knows it
speaks   in his own voice
or tries to,
his words encoded,
body raised
over the frozen earth.
Too late.
The rest are passengers,
sad romantic
pilgrims. Listen!
To want to take a walk
at midnight
or at two o'clock
is pushing back the time.
The hour hand
spins crazily,
the numbers on its face,

burning like stars,
turn red.
He is the friend of Harry Heine,
they assure us.
Let him speak.

THE COSMOS IN HIS MIND, CONCEALED

Someone is geared to go,
but holds back,
holds the cosmos
in his mind,
concealed,
the dark side of the image
still too deep
for thought, prefigured
by a cruel
intelligence.
He is the friend of someone
older, caught between
his world & yours,
no end to what
he sees,
the world's immensity
still smaller
than that other world
in its black hole.
"Release me."
"Feed me."
Whose design this is
they do not know,
but cling to cyberspace
as if it held
a clue   the outline
of a village
filled with snow
or circumstance.
The wise man runs from it,
like poetry
or dreams.
The ones he leaves behind
pick up the shards.

THE MOST REMARKABLE
OBSTRUCTIONS

In the last book
written, words
move slowly,
falter   halfway down
the page, impede
the flow,
sentences we might have spoken
but held back,
tarried until our eyes,
used to the light,
captured them written.
Misted eyeglasses,
the sugar at the bottom of
his cup   he waits
until the year spills over
like a day,
the time from here to here
minus an hour,
sight unseen,
the most remarkable
obstructions,
snagging,
turning *brown & hard.*
Somewhere a mountain crumbles
in the mind   an ocean
breaking through
buries the dead terrain.
The word he hears
—*impedimenta*—
is almost too much to bear.
It melts like wax
when written,
covers the space between
his eyes & yours.
Out of the mud

a street grows flowers.
Stones lie buried
where they fell.
He leaves a poem for us
entitled   *after the flood.*

THE BURDEN OF ALL POETRY

To speak in his own voice
is painful now
the vowel half concealed
in what the other poet
speaks   *in silent icicles*
quietly shining to
the quiet moon   (S.T. Coleridge)
the burden of all poetry
they called romantic.
Sometimes solitary, sometimes
in the green flood
only pretending to be
solitary   right is left,
the hand that rocks the cradle
forfeits the shocks of love.
"She eats & wipes her mouth,"
a gesture that goes by
so fast, so little to be seen
we might have fainted
in anticipation.
Two by two by two
the crowd around the table
stabilizes. Forfeiture
was never clearer,
never like what the hands,
strapped to the dead man's sides,
kept hidden.
I am that I am,
he says at last,
like Popeye
or the lord god
of their prophets,
lately revealed,
awakening,
ready to deal
a fatal hand.

HIS IS THE SOUND PERENNIAL

He is his father's
father   *what a strange*
relationship
their thoughts of derring-do
illumining the past,
the question always
gnawing at them:
do these sentences make sense?
In the nether hole
where white & black collide
the sense of space
escapes him.
It is 8:00 a.m in Paris
& still dark.
The narrow road leads to
annihilation,
yet has the brilliance
of a birthday,
remembering how happily
the words once came,
the ease of being
what their fathers called
a man. *Toujours.*
His is the sound perennial,
the thought that contradicts
itself, the lie
that leads them to the truth.
Be seated.
You have reached a certain age
unknown to those
before you.
Twice a man   twice blest
in holy weather
you will become like us
the one who guards the secret
lodged in your throat.

A GATHERING OF POETS

Hidden in sleep
a gathering of poets
—not a paradise—
will lead us
backwards
toward a crack
in time, will make
the flight
down to the lost lagoon
a rite of passage.
What could be finer
for a man,
than wrestling with his demons,
half with smiles,
the other half of him
in mourning?
Laughing in the face of death
he feels his life,
this conduit for
unseen worlds,
dormant inside him,
struggling awake.
The man who was his brother
shows him an ugly lip,
too awful for the others
to abide. The luckless poets
ride on air   a world
strewn with a chain of roads,
black reservoirs,
white buildings,
spreading below them.
Night sky hides
the earth.
A tower hides a roof.
The flicker of a movie
is so cruel

their eyes will soon grow blind
with visions,
helpless to see.

CRACKED SHADOWS

A street of men in black,
cracked shadows,
come forth from every
doorway, stragglers
to the call of god
& country, they are neither
yours nor ours,
neither meat nor milk.
Something in the eyes
of some, some hint
pregnant with promise,
is enough to mask
the mystery of men
with robes & beards
black as the sun
that lights their Sabbath.
Going from darkness to
a well-lit room
a perpendicular arrangement
sends them flying.
Silk hidden under linen
breaks their law.
When they reclaim
their eyes
nothing remains
but faded petals,
stamens no longer
green, not natural   (after Goethe)
but fantasies
rosettes   in stone
carved by
a master hand.

ROMANTIC DADAS

for Jeffrey Robinson

A late night party
where Romantic Dadas
cut a rug   too iridescent
to resist
our smug caresses.
How will we begin
addressing them,
by name or by a face
that turns away from you
unseen, leaves scarce
a trace behind.
Mister Novalis,
or if that isn't
your real name,
drop it right now
& try another.
He is too determined,
too far below
his average height
for anyone to count.
Aside from which
there are the odors
of the women
who surround him,
so many that the walls begin
to press his skull.
He has to break away
to make an outcry
in the name of Dada.
I & I & I are left
without a place
ulterior to place,
to run or hide.

THE PERSISTENCE OF
THE LYRIC VOICE
for Scott McLean

He will keep writing,
will he not,
as you will.
A pressure like a finger
builds inside
his chest
& travels upward,
somewhere between
the trachea
& glottis,
pushes the fold aside
& breaks.
Imagined speech.
It is the same for everything
we say   we think we know
the speaker but the speaker
escapes our observation.
It is this concealment
that reveals
the truth of poetry
no less authoritative
than the other
in full gusto.
From the direction of his voice,
an absence & a grief,
his profile is a kind of blue.
The footfall of a wanderer
crosses the open field
in daylight.
Let the *spirit* rise
until it's *mind,*
the untranslated,
untranslatable,
in which the lyric voice

resides   mind's matter
& its coming forth
by day.

OF DANCERS & MAGICIANS
for Emmett Williams

The music that a man
raps out,
slapping his hands
against his shiny
skull, how it can
summon us to join
the company
of dancers & magicians.
Each with a Polish
mother, we can count
the time between
the silences, the memories
that mask our turnings.
Love, like intelligence,
opens a door,
to let us in
still blind
& searching,
taking as a sign
the names of God
engraved in
amethyst   a counterfeit
infinity,
not letting time
pretend to halt
the darker flux,
impediment to where
we set our sights.
Here is a place to hang
a flag, & there a hat
to pull a flag from.
All your little men
are watching,
waking from a dream.
There is no predicting
summer
but it always comes.

AMONG THE LESSER LIGHTS

Ups-a-daisy like a word
no one will speak
again   the thought
that everything we know
will soon be history.
Among the lesser lights
a dog is sinking
in the mud,
the way we suffer
without sound
or sustenance.
The predators fan out,
heavy with premonitions,
mindful of their role
as pawns
& patriots.
Redeemed the mother cries
her head held high
marking a final crossing
to a foreign land.
The fact that after
a whole lifetime
nothing has been resolved
catches in her throat.
She reaches out a hand,
as we do,
praying for the silence,
for the accolades
to cease.
The circle, brown
& edging
into yellow,
starts to swell   moistens
& leaves a trail of fat.

A SINGLE MOMENT, CALLED A LIFE

The simple pleasures,
one by one,
that walking in a city
often brings,
how can we count them
when they hide from us?
Particular as three o'clock
the sound is not a sound
but wraps us in an air
of silence   stepping out
one foot before the other
in the dying light.
Are we prepared at last
to end, to kick
the stool aside,
here where we stand
& count the centuries,
where time compresses
to a single moment
called a life?
The man who waits here
has no eyes,
his eyebrows hang
below his chin.
He tells us: this
is everything
& this is nothing.
I also could not become
a phoenix.   (Shun'oku Myooha 1311–1388)

THE DARKNESS THAT SURROUNDS US

for Robert Creeley

A night sky clear
but empty   time
bereft of stars
the darkness that sur-
rounds us darker
still.
    Forsaken
gazing skywards where
the moon once shone,
a line of planets
locked in place
forever
the rest unseen.
To end in dark-
ness is their surest
wish, *the horrible*
in every particle of air,
submerged in droplets—
vision!
But the eye is never
more than what one
life can hold,
the emptiness expanding
forever out of reach,
the sun devouring
her children.
One who never was a prophet
is.
The final
Armageddon will arrive
when there is no one
left to see
or to be seen.

WHERE ALL LIGHT IS ABSENT

                                    Taking
                              a
                        further
                  step
              then
          falling
      back,
repining
where too much
light is,
blindness
as black as night
must follow,
& where all light
is absent,
blindness
must follow too,
the sun extinguish'd   (for Lord Byron in the
rayless, pathless,   Wilderness)
& the icy earth
turned blind & blackening
in the moonless air—
the words of one
you could not
fathom   sad   prophetic
striding through
his wilderness
& weathered,
tethered to
the time to come.

THE RESORT TO AMBER

|1| *small birds in fragments*
overhead   the lapse of what
was once a landscape,
terminal its name
& frequent
the resort to amber.
|2| Faces flash across
the screen   they vanish,
so little to report
or scan,
the harsh facts
frozen under thumb,
prone to return
& numb you.
|3| Alphabet is blest,
the source of
everything we know,
its spell a power
& a curse.
|4| The short way out
is through
the middle door,
the street
below, the garden
to one side,
a line of *stones*
whose particles are toads   (C. Smart)
polished & clean.
|5| The flies over your heads
are feckless   buzzing barely
until they die.

CONCEALED ASSASSINS

Those who are masters
needn't talk,
but signal with a secret
nod or wink,
concealed assassins
brought into the mix.
Involuntary tears,
a dream of executions,   (C. Baudelaire)
smoke
rises between our teeth.
The ones who loved us
die   not one by one
but now *en masse,*
the presence of the dead
in every corner.
The wretch who testifies
may also sing,
capturing the ebb & flow
of tides, the pressure
blood breeds
where it stokes the body.
Once to stand there,
hapless,
to sense the joy
in failure
only the wise
can know.
Someone will lift
a burden
from our eyes
& we will witness
worlds unseen.

THE MOON INSANE & FEEBLE

Loony moon, whose babies
suck a ring,
how many look to you
or look beyond you?
Little dolls, like
clockwork, pumping
air & beckoning,
are what the man pretends
to cherish. Halfway
up the stairs,
the window brings him
to the sky,
the sky to where
the moon
insane & feeble
hides   a white   (P.B. Shelley)
& shapeless mass.
Pleasure that should be his
escapes him,
he is always
in pursuit,
always the distant runner.
A flock of moons,
the leaden weight
of butterflies
oppresses him.
To wait there,
dewy eyed,
to write the final line,
how long before
life breaks,
before what's written
fades from sight.
A song sounds
in the mind
& quavers:

Cold is hot
(he cries)
but hot
is never cold.

DIFFERENCES ARE GOOD

Differences are good,
writes Hölderlin,
a yellow lake,
a cairn of senseless
stones, embellishments
too old to keep
in mind, the voices
spinning in the air
of distant speakers.
They will have made
your day, not
for the first time,
omnipotent but wistful,
who have dug
their heels, weary
with marching,
into your carpets.
Listening, alive
& careless,
the news brought
to your screen
void of content
that will further conceal
what afflicts you.
The darkness more than
half the universe,
a word like *shivered*
can't contain it.
March in time.
Retreat.
A loss of place.
Surprisingly.
Reclining.
Only death will set us free.

THE REST IS LEFT TO CHANCE

Only death will set us free,
the rest is left
to chance.
Inside the house,
its walls down,
ground into a dust
that only the dream
sustains, those
who were once alive
do not arise,
but *one by one*
by snakes   (T.L. Beddoes)
their limbs are swallowed.
Almost enough
to make you
suffocate, to lodge
like mercury
under your tongue.
A dark car
rides along
a white road
wild with rain.
The pain it sparks
will never leave you,
not by chance
& not by force of will,
but irretrievable
will burn on
hard & gem-like.
Fathers as young as you
once sensed it,
their dread a provocation
to persist.

WHAT THE SONG REVEALS

Turn it aside
& live with it—
an empty
stupid (M. Lermontov)
joke,
like life itself,
like memory.
The intercessors ride you,
what they hide is what
the song reveals:
a catch deep in your throat,
blocking the words
without which
nothing can endure
more sure than love.
Romanticism is the name
he gives it,
only to have it falter
like all names
before it.
Everyone is old,
he thinks,
but I am older,
pouring secrecy upon
the dying page, (G. Corso)
a step the young
take as they start
to vanish.
They are the ones
who face you,
not for the sake
of beauty
but in the mind's
demise.

A TALE OF FURTIVE MOVEMENTS

for Hiroaki Sato, in memoriam Yukio Mishima

Sly enough to hide
his slyness,   (D. Solomos)
he is almost
another animal,
somewhere between
a snake & rabbit,
the very opposite of what
men take for granted.
Men who are in love
with men, dissemblers,
leave us no slack.
They tell a tale
of furtive movements,
even now,
the prince of tides
eager to die,
who will *not* put the sword
aside, but fervent,
in the sight of all,
plunges until the hilt
is all that's left.
The earthquake hidden
underneath the ground
is ever present.
It is what leads
the man, stripped
to his skin,
to take the final
plunge
unknown to you
before the beauty of
his face & limbs,
so treasured,
leaves him, degraded
in the dust.

THE ORACLE,
IF WE CAN CALL IT THAT

for Hannah Weiner

Until we fade
into our last
concealment, never
anything more real
than this,
we wait & then
at last we see
the words,
the screen,
the ink spread in
a silver wash,
the glow.
I am the ogre, then—
he writes—   (V. Hugo)
I am the scapegoat.
The oracle,
if we can call it that,
hides in the words,
the words obscure
the other words,
each word among us
is a harbinger,
called by a number
like the fingers
on one hand.
The numbers written
on the rims of wheels
also are letters,
never added up,
but intersecting in a frenzy
each upon each.

TO TAKE DEATH AS A TRIBUTE
(A VARIATION)

for Will Alexander

Our dreams were of suns,
of vermilion dragons
spangled with gold
from Sumeria,
pronouncements & omens
concealed, to take death
as a tribute,
a slave plunged
in water
& drowning,
becoming a wife
to their god,
a scorpion,
then a chimera.
They were prey to
maneuverings,
played them with zeal,
to no end
that they knew,
to declare new beginnings,
bestriding a sand dune,
vacuums a god might
transform to a cosmos,
infinity's mirror,
a place internal to place,
a procedure a king
once devised,
divination from innards,
a rapturous babble.

SHE IS ALPHA & HE IS OMEGA
(A SECOND VARIATION)

for Will Alexander

In a fusion
of boundaries & cores
she is Venus
to whom we do homage,
whose sleek apparition
still guides us:
encirclements first
& transgressions
to follow.
She is Alpha
& he is Omega,
a being, a deity
carried by priests
& by people
costumed as demons.
A glass shatters,
time ends,
& consciousness
blazing with suns
flows & ebbs.
O Marduk
creator of cultures
& crimes,
whose mind is a void,
who is forever deaf
to our voicings.

THE PAST UNCOVERED

Strange how his voice
now sounds
like someone else's,
or how change,
once rare,
comes quicker,
overwhelms us
day by day.
The past uncovered
years ago
closes again.
The sky is white,
all color drained from it,
or black,
percussion sounding
in percussion's
wake, the screen
of dancing letters,
broken, splintering
the light.
The first word spoken
is a hermit's
cry, the words
that follow burst
your eardrums.
History is over.
In another world
you find another
young as you,
your shadow
over his, the two
together, sharing
hidden sorrows,
thoughts of   (G. de Nerval)
expiation. The world
does not forgive.

THE FIRST WORD SPOKEN

The first word
spoken, not
a word
erupts, full blown
& linked
to passages of terror,
breaking from
the gullet,
cries a crow makes
or a distant
relative, an uncle
lost to time.
He waits surrounded
by an empty night,
a wind of noise   (D.G. Rossetti)
that is alone
like God   that has
the sky in it.
Tempestuous & terror-
stricken, he is forced
to speak. He does
& somehow runs,
recoils into his mind,
poor voyager,
the word not yet a word,
a sigh, a murmur,
tongue & teeth
at odds,
& lips through which
saliva dribbles,
one cry linking
with another   syntax
before speech,
the word still hidden,
waiting to be born.

A GAME OF ULTIMATE
CONCEALMENTS

In old age
they grew young,
iridescent,
letting the years
fly by.
Inside the dormitory
trees took root.
The soil, black
in your hand,
reflected
your own demise,
a hole through which
dead time slid,
never to be redeemed.
Unseen, unknown,
the universe was lost
in darkness.
In a game of ultimate
concealments, who
came out ahead,
who more than you
succumbed to time?
Too deep for tears   (W. Wordsworth)
the clock inside the brain
goes crazy.
The elders wait
& curse their young,
too eager to retreat,
too much like clowns
or emperors.
Lift the hammer
& over your head
lift the icecap.
A door centers the light
& frames it.
Shut it tight.

TO COUNT TIME FROM THE FUTURE

Keepers of that
great romance   (E. Dickinson)
foreclosed to us
like stumble bums,
the light erupts
again   again
cleaving the darkness,
then subsides.
Time is beyond the call
of time, beyond
whatever led us,
fed us while we slept,
unable to turn back.
A year of war
won't end it,
once we know the rules,
the game, the hatred
spurning love,
the burden of our songs
thrown back at us.
The dead, too long
ignored, rise up,
their cries immaculate
& freed of sense,
who show rare beauty
where the flesh
drops off.
Too many overtures
clutter the air.
The rage for new
beginnings, starts
clashing with
the storied past,
the time of the assassins
never more near
than now.

To count time from
the future
offers us
little choice.

THE BRAIN TURNED UPSIDE DOWN

To count time from
the future,
having the end
in view,
this is a sore reminder
of another world,
another chance
to come into the open air,
out of the darkness.
The brain turned upside
down, they told us,
gathers no moss.
No clash of symbols
half as painful
as discounted
time, ready
to plug us
one by one.
A star most spiritual,
preeminent,   (G.M. Hopkins)
of all the golden press,
where what is dark
is not obscure,
leads rather
to another light,
a revelation
of the end of all.
For this things fly away,
the distance between
one & one
becomes a universe
no one will track.
The time to view the stars
grows scarce,
the farther we look...
A walk across the street
reckons infinity
& more.

AND THEREFORE PERSONAL

Rage dies
slowly
but it dies
& no one here
retrieves it
since it's yours
& therefore
personal   a mark
from birth
filling your mouth
with ice
a cold rage
in a hot month
often enough
repeated
& more than pain
the sparks fly
like a vision
not to be reduced
or tempered,
raging high above,
bombs set free
in clusters
the open city
hostage to a lie
the plazas
crammed with ghosts
with babes
as pale as water
& a woman's voice
enraged   tests time
& bellows:
I am starving for
this feast
& I know where sleeps   (A.I. Menken)
Holofernes.

NOUS LES SENTONS PARTOUT

Nothing held back
but spoken
in another voice,
another country
where words
ring false.
So soon forgotten,
wrapped away.
The truth of revelation
is the truth
of revelation lost
& nothing less.
Nous les sentons
partout   lumières bleus
nous les voyons
flotter   les appelons
nos morts.
The truth of what
our eyes can't see
the final truth
concealed in darkness,
not a god
& not a harbinger
of light.
A murmur slipping
toward silence,   (C. Norwid)
the heady turmoil
of a meal
served in the dark,
the smell of sex
fresh on your fingers.
Every window
on this street
fills up with light
yet no one marks us,
no one foretells

the heartbeat
under gauze.
Forlorn.
A mystery
even the dead
can't salve.+

                  + solve

HOW CAN THIS BE TRUE?

After concealments, all
lies open.
No one still falls for it
& no one can escape
the guilt at having
turned aside.
The liar rules.
Abandoned by his friends,
the thrill of something
sexual   a glove
a ring of feathers
stars aligned
& throbbing   how
can this be true?
The friends who died
stay dead   the lovers
turn to ghosts
& vanish.
That funny word
alas sometimes
disturbs us.
It is a hoverer,
a vestige of the past
erased & dead,
tempted to push it
under, hidden,
cached, erased,
eroded, rotten.
If a friend   robbed
of his intuition
perishes, what choice
remains to us?
For this the questions,
bottomless, proceed
by turns.

A snowy truculus,
fluttering in rocky hell,　　　　　(T.L. Beddoes)
murders its young
& dies.

HIS FINAL DAYS

he is a real man
when he murders,
is he not?
the poem concludes
or does it?
in the nick of someone's
time, the later years
emerging helter-
skelter,
lines
constricted
into single
words
the witness spews,
the sick taste
sticking in
his craw,
his orange tongue
unraveling,
picking through the gravel.
Perish warmth,
he writes,
Old age: "the Shape   (S.T. Coleridge)
& Messenger
of Death."
A book they call
The War Years
signals his final days,
looking for respite,
half afraid he is
to waiver, to be
written off & sealed.
What was real once
is real no longer,
the man betrayed
by hope

has little left
but fear itself.
It finds a place
near to his heart,
starts racing through
his limbs & loins,
conjoined to all
he cherishes,
then brings him down.

IN THE BOOK OF CONCEALMENTS

everything is concealed,
therefore the book
runs out   the pages
still glued together
must be torn
apart. Hello again,
dear little dove,
we have agreed to be
your crazed pursuers.
Standing on a pebbled beach,
the sand pushed back,
thousands of shining
jellyfish obstruct
our passage.
We have to strain
to read,
the letters even now
escaping, twisting
back & forth,
the world so soon
engulfed.
In the book of concealments
on the final page
we find the secret written,
words askew,
a distant swarm of hummers
darkening the land.
The armies never stop.
The men who fish
are fishers,
draw their lines across,
two threads, one side
in red
one side in black,
the eye of man
shut tight.

What are the words they proffer,
paper thin?
"You are the prince of waters"
reads the missive.
"I have loved you."

POSTSCRIPT TO
A BOOK OF CONCEALMENTS

There is a burnt book
that remains a book,

a hidden book
which, if it opened,

would tear the walls
of time down, let

the false world
infiltrate &

overwhelm
the real.

June 2008

J erome Rothenberg, internationally known poet/translator/editor/essayist, is the author of more than eighty volumes of published poetry, a dozen important books of translations, and ten groundbreaking anthologies of contemporary and traditional poetry, including *Technicians of the Sacred* and, with Pierre Joris and Jeffrey C. Robinson, *Poems for the Millennium* in three volumes.

TITLES FROM BLACK WIDOW PRESS

TRANSLATION SERIES

Approximate Man and Other Writings
by Tristan Tzara. Translated and edited
by Mary Ann Caws.

Art Poétique
by Guillevic. Translated by Maureen Smith.

Capital of Pain
by Paul Eluard. Translated by Mary Ann Caws,
Patricia Terry, and Nancy Kline.

Chanson Dada: Selected Poems
by Tristan Tzara. Translated with an introduction
and essay by Lee Harwood.

Essential Poems and Writings of Joyce Mansour:
A Bilingual Anthology
Translated with an introduction by
Serge Gavronsky.

Essential Poems and Writings of Robert Desnos:
A Bilingual Anthology
Edited with an introduction and essay
by Mary Ann Caws.

EyeSeas (Les Ziaux)
by Raymond Queneau. Translated with
an introduction by Daniela Hurezanu and
Stephen Kessler.

The Inventor of Love & Other Writings
by Gherasim Luca. Translated by Julian
and Laura Semilian. Introduction by
Andrei Codrescu. Essay by Petre Răileanu.

La Fontaine's Bawdy
by Jean de la Fontaine. Translated with an
introduction by Norman R. Shapiro.

Last Love Poems of Paul Eluard
Translated with an introduction by
Marilyn Kallet.

Love, Poetry (L'amour la poésie)
by Paul Eluard. Translated with an essay
by Stuart Kendall.

Poems of André Breton: A Bilingual Anthology
Translated with essays by Jean-Pierre
Cauvin and Mary Ann Caws.

Poems of A.O. Barnabooth
by Valéry Larbaud. Translated by
Ron Padgett and Bill Zavatsky.

Preversities: A Jacques Prévert Sampler
Translated and edited by Norman R. Shapiro.

The Sea and Other Poems
by Guillevic. Translated by Patricia Terry.
Introduction by Monique Chefdor.

To Speak, to Tell You?
Poems by Sabine Sicaud. Translated by
Norman R. Shapiro. Introduction and notes
by Odile Ayral-Clause.

forthcoming translations

Essential Poems and Prose of Jules Laforgue
Translated and edited by Patricia Terry.

Essential Poems and Writings of Pierre Reverdy
Translated by Mary Ann Caws and
Patricia Terry.

Furor and Mystery & Other Writings
by René Char. Edited and translated by
Mary Ann Caws and Nancy Kline.

I Want No Part in It and Other Writings
by Benjamin Péret. Translated with an
introduction by James Brook.

The Big Game
by Benjamin Péret. Translated with an
introduction by Marilyn Kallet.

A Life of Poems, Poems of a Life
by Anna de Noailles. Translated by Norman
R. Shapiro. Introduction by Catherine Perry.

MODERN POETRY SERIES

An Alchemist with One Eye on Fire
by Clayton Eshleman

Anticline
by Clayton Eshleman

Archaic Design
by Clayton Eshleman

Backscatter: New and Selected Poems
by John Olson

The Caveat Onus
by Dave Brinks. The complete cycle,
four volumes in one.

Concealments and Caprichos
by Jerome Rothenberg

Crusader-Woman
by Ruxandra Cesereanu. Translated
by Adam J. Sorkin. Introduction by
Andrei Codrescu.

Fire Exit
by Robert Kelly

Forgiven Submarine
by Ruxandra Cesereanu and
Andrei Codrescu

The Grindstone of Rapport:
A Clayton Eshleman Reader
Forty years of poetry, prose, and
translations by Clayton Eshleman.

Packing Light: New and Selected Poems
by Marilyn Kallet

Signal from Draco: New and Selected Poems
by Mebane Robertson

forthcoming
modern poetry titles

Curdled Skulls: Poems of Bernard Bador
Translated by Clayton Eshleman and Bernard
Bador.

from stone this running
by Heller Levinson

Larynx Galaxy
by John Olson

Present Tense of the World: Poems 2000–2008
by Amina Saïd. Translated by Marilyn Hacker.

Exile is My Trade: A Habib Tengour Reader
Translated by Pierre Joris.

LITERARY THEORY / BIOGRAPHY SERIES

Revolution of the Mind:
The Life of André Breton
by Mark Polizzotti. Revised
and augmented edition.

WWW.BLACKWIDOWPRESS.COM